Mountain Brook Baptist Church in Birmingham, Alabama, presents this
collection of devotions in honor of our beloved pastor, Dr. Doug Dortch,
upon his retirement as our senior minister 2011–2021, and in appreciation for
his exemplary ministry during the COVID-19 crisis of 2020–2021.

HAVE A MINUTE?

Devotional Thoughts in a Season of Challenges

Doug Dortch

© 2021
Published in the United States by Nurturing Faith, Macon, GA.
Nurturing Faith is a book imprint of Good Faith Media (goodfaithmedia.org).
Library of Congress Cataloging-in-Publication Data is available.

ISBN: 978-1-63528-157-6

All scripture citations are from the New Revised International Version (NRSV)
unless otherwise indicated.

Dedication

To the members of the Mountain Brook Baptist Church, who have never ceased to astound me with their grace and generosity... Every crisis contains numerous opportunities, and every challenge affords us the chance to put our best foot forward. I am most proud of our church and our ministerial staff, who stepped forward to seize the moment and did so most faithfully for God's glory, not our own. You have "redeemed the times" (Eph. 5:16). Well done, good and faithful servants.

Contents

EASTERTIDE

ORDINARY TIME

Preface

March 15 is famously known as the Ides of March. That phrase come to us from Shakespeare's play, *Julius Caesar*, in which as he describes the impending assassination of the emperor, a random fortuneteller calls out to Caesar from among the crowd: "Beware the Ides of March" (Act 1, Scene 2, 15-19).

For us at Mountain Brook Baptist Church, March 15 marked a different kind of foreboding, one that began a season of shutdown in which, due to a raging virus, we found our rhythms and relationships suddenly interrupted. The threat of infection from the coronavirus, COVID-19, brought so much of life's activities, including gathered worship, to a screeching halt. Like Julius Caesar, we never saw such an interruption coming.

When it did, however, our church's ministerial staff quickly scrambled to determine how best to keep our church together during a shutdown whose duration we could not have predicted. Activities quickly shifted from in-person to online, and a host of digital content became posted to our church's various social media accounts as a way to maintain important connections. One of those digital initiatives was a daily devotion I began almost immediately, called "Have a Minute?" Its purpose was simply to offer a brief thought each weekday that might inspire and encourage participants to hold fast to their faith in a season where so much else seemed to be unraveling. Little did I imagine how much traction those devotions would get and how wide their reach would become.

As with many other digital offerings our church's ministerial staff produced, Mountain Brook Baptist Church extended its reach exponentially. What once was a congregation that based its ministries on attracting people to our physical location at the corner of Montevallo and Overbrook roads (just as did most other congregations in their contexts), Mountain Brook suddenly became a "light to the nations," literally speaking, as our witness went out to a much larger audience around the world.

This book is a collection of some of those daily devotions. The idea of compiling these offerings in written form came from a group of lay leaders in our church who thought these writings might benefit an even larger number of readers, looking for spiritual support long after COVID has gone (or until the next pandemic arrives). I am flattered and humbled that they would think these musings might have a "shelf life" long after they were first delivered.

In addition to expressing my appreciation to our church's lay leaders for this initiative, I also wish to thank David Hull and Susan Hull Walker and the William E. and Wylodine H. Hull Memorial Fund for providing the funds for this publication.

ADVENT

Walk in the Name of the LORD

Micah 4:5

All the nations may walk in the name of their gods,
but we will walk in the name of the LORD GOD for ever and ever.

In the days before COVID one of the more popular fund-raising activities was to organize a walk to promote attention to some important cause. Of course, if the cause was political, then you would call the walk a "march." But "walk" or "march," they're essentially the same thing. If enough people can come together around a common cause and show their support to it, then maybe they can create a larger movement, one that might change the culture for the better.

I'm not against that form of free speech. It is, after all, one guaranteed in our Constitution's Bill of Rights. But what if there might be a way that people of faith join together to create a movement in the direction of God, a movement that might make our world more of what God created it to be?

That's the type of movement the prophet Micah was working toward in his prophecy. Micah, a contemporary of the prophet Isaiah, envisioned a day when people from the surrounding nations would be streaming in God's direction to learn of God's ways and to walk in his paths. In preparation for that great day, what the prophets referred to as the "Day of the LORD," Micah thought it important for people of faith to begin immediately to order their lives in anticipation of that good future. He saw it as a protest against the prevailing culture and a manifestation of the better way of life that living for God makes possible. In the fourth chapter, Micah says, "All the nations may walk in the name of their gods; we will walk in the name of the LORD our God forever and ever."

It's not hard to see how people today are chasing the wrong things and going in the wrong direction. They lack any sense of meaning or purpose to their lives. They're walking after gods that cannot sustain them. But what difference might it make if they could see an example of someone who walks with God and, by doing so, adds so much to their life? What difference might it make if they could see that in you?

So, today, watch where you're walking and pay attention to whom you're following. If you find that you're walking any path except the path of righteousness, change your direction before it's too late. Only then will your future be one of favor and blessing, the sort of abundance God always makes possible for those who promote his cause and are careful to order their every step in his name.

The Blessing of Smallness
Micah 5:2

But you, Bethlehem Ephrathah, though you are small among the clans of Judah,
out of you will come for me one who will be ruler over Israel,
whose origins are from of old, from ancient times.

If there's a motto by which our prevailing culture seems to live, it's this: "Bigger is better." That's true of businesses and schools and even churches. If something has size, we also think it has substance. But that's not always so.

It's a good thing that it's not always so. Some of us aren't in a position to experience bigness. Some of us aren't born into this world with the advantages that give us a head start on others. Some of us do the best that we can, but others always seem to be passing us by. Some of us seem to be cursed with perpetual littleness.

But in Micah's prophecy we are reminded of how one of the beautiful parts of the Christmas story is the way God chose something small and seemingly insignificant to be the means for sending his son into the world. One of the great prophecies Jesus fulfilled was the one about which we read in the fifth chapter of Micah's prophecy. It goes like this: "But you, Bethlehem Ephrathah, though you are small among the clans of Judah, out of you will come for me one who will be ruler over Israel." The "little town of Bethlehem" was the place God chose to be the birthplace of Christ, the Messiah.

God is always confounding the strong and the wise by his choice of the weak and the foolish. God's righteousness is not always determined by mere arithmetic. Sometimes God employs the little things in this world so that we might apprehend his work only with eyes of faith. Sometimes God does this so that we might not elevate accomplishments over grace and merit over mercy. Sometimes God uses the seemingly insignificant things to help us see that unless we become dependent upon him as a little child, even a Bethlehem baby, we'll never see the kingdom of heaven.

As you sing Christmas carols in this most blessed season and come to the classic, "O Little Town of Bethlehem," say a silent prayer for how God used such an out-of-the-way place to be the entry point for our Savior and LORD. Think also of how God might use little you in some holy way during this Advent season to point others to Jesus in much the same way.

Serving While We Wait

1 Thessalonians 1:7-10

And so you became a model to all the believers in Macedonia and Achaia. The LORD's message rang out from you not only in Macedonia and Achaia—your faith in God has become known everywhere. Therefore we do not need to say anything about it, for they themselves report what kind of reception you gave us. They tell how you turned to God from idols to serve the living and true God, and to wait for his Son from heaven, whom he raised from the dead—Jesus, who rescues us from the coming wrath.

One of the hardest parts of the Christian faith for those of us who tend to be driven people is learning how to be patient and knowing how best to wait. This lesson is especially tough during a time like Advent, which puts a premium on waiting. The focus of Advent is of course on knowing how to keep our eyes and hearts pealed on Jesus' second coming, but we seem to find a way to make it into a monthlong Christmas celebration instead of a time to prepare ourselves for Jesus' return. Certainly, there is a connection between Jesus' first coming at Christmas and his second coming in God's future, but if we only give attention to one part of that connection, we are weaker in our discipleship for it.

Waiting is tough, particularly if we are constitutionally inclined toward action. But it may be that for those of us who are wired that way, the Apostle Paul gives us some direction in his first letter to the Thessalonians—the earliest of Paul's epistles. Written roughly two decades after Jesus' death and resurrection, it seeks to offer encouragement to believers who had become weary of waiting for Jesus to return.

In 1 Thessalonians 1, Paul lauds the church for how they were a model congregation for churches everywhere through the manner in which they were, as we might call them, "actively waiting." Paul writes, "We don't really need to say anything about your good example, because those churches themselves testify to how you turned to God from idols to serve the living and true God and to wait for his Son from heaven, who he raised from the dead—Jesus who rescues us from the coming wrath." In other words, these Thessalonians weren't just twiddling their thumbs while they were waiting for Jesus to return. They were serving God, which made their waiting more purposeful and more obedient.

Today, you'll more than likely not have much of a chance to be standing around waiting for Jesus to return. You've got too much on your plate. But what if you went about your affairs with a heart bent on serving God? Even if what you have going on is consumed by Christmas preparation, what if you were to go about it as a way of bearing witness to your faith in Christ? I'd say you'd then be waiting with a purpose; you'd be putting your faith to work. And I'd say that if Jesus were to return, he'd be pleased with your witness, so pleased that he would in fact be coming to save you from "the coming wrath."

No Wrong Turns

Psalm 85.8-9

I will listen to what God the LORD says;
he promises peace to his people, his faithful servants
—but let them not turn to folly.
Surely his salvation is near those who fear him,
that his glory may dwell in our land.

As we move toward the second Sunday in Advent, we focus our attention on God's promise of peace. Peace, as the Bible defines it, points to a life of well-being, one that is marked by both calmness and confidence. But it's not a self-centered calmness and confidence; it's instead one that is grounded in one's faith in God.

Psalm 85 helps us to see and appreciate the difference between the two. A self-centered calmness and confidence are what the Psalmist refers to as based in "folly" because of how it is not sufficiently located in God's guidance. "I will listen to what God the LORD will say; he promises peace to his people, but let them not return to folly." In other words, when people choose to go their own way instead of God's way, they have chosen foolishly because they have set out on a course that will inevitably take them in a direction away from God, one that will surely be marked by all manner of chaos and confusion. Only by following God's path will we be assured of God's protection and provisions, an assurance that will sustain us even when things seem to be unsettled.

Think of the angel's instruction to the shepherds of Bethlehem in Luke's gospel, where they are told that "this day in the town of David a Savior has been born to you, he is Christ the LORD." When they saw the heavenly hosts praising God and saying, "Glory to God in the highest and on earth, peace to men on whom God's favor rests," the shepherds were of one mind to "go to Bethlehem and see this thing that has come to pass, which the LORD has told us about." Their faith fulfilled the heart of the Psalmist: "Surely his salvation is near those who fear him that his glory may dwell in our land" (Ps. 85:9).

Today, listen to what God says and do what God gives you to do. Then you will glorify God and know the peace God promises, a peace that will guide you in making the right turns in life and will secure for you the full measure of God's salvation.

The Desire of Our Hearts

Isaiah 26:8

Yes, LORD, walking in the way of your laws, we wait for you;
your name and renown are the desire of our hearts.

I've always been a tad suspicious of those who constantly speak about how the Bible promises people of faith the desires of our heart. I know there are many places where we are told that God will grant us such a thing. But the problem lies in our interpretation of that promise and in particular how we tend to wrench it out of context so that we fail to see it in connection with our making sure that our desires match God's desires.

For example, in Isaiah 26 we see the "desires of our heart" language showing up, though in the context of walking in God's ways and waiting for God to reveal himself to us. For Isaiah, that walking and waiting meant calling a backsliding people to return to a life of obedience, a life marked by doing God's will and not expecting God to put his divine stamp of approval on theirs. Only then would God secure their future and glorify his name in the process.

The Christmas season is all about bending toward Bethlehem and elevating the Christ-child whose name means "God is our salvation." It's about aligning our lives with God's redemptive purposes and showing the world how those purposes have been uniquely and definitely fulfilled in the person of Jesus.

Yes, in the Christmas season there's a lot of talk about "what do you want for Santa to bring?" I'm not against presents or Christmas gifts. But I do think it's important for us to consider what God might want to receive from us, which is our full obedience. Then we would make sure that our desires rightly line up with God's so that we might walk on his level and smooth path, always waiting for God to lead and never getting ahead of him in any way.

Strive to Become God's Pride and Glory

Isaiah 4:2-3

In that day the Branch of the LORD will be beautiful and glorious, and the fruit of the land will be the pride and glory of the survivors in Israel. Those who are left in Zion, who remain in Jerusalem, will be called holy, all who are recorded among the living in Jerusalem.

Now that I'm a grandparent, I find that I'm as prone to brag on my grandchildren as any grandparent worth his salt. There once was a time when as a mere parent I would tell myself that once my children began having children, I'd find a way to be more restrained than most grandparents. But of course, I've been a miserable failure in that regard, and truth be told, I'm quite proud of it.

As I've thought about my own response to grandparenting, I think it has something to do with feeling good about your family's future and your own sense of accomplishment at producing offspring whom you hope will make even greater contributions to society than you. Maybe I'm reading too much into it, but I don't think so. It's not just about their success; it's also about your success through those who come behind you.

That hope for a future legacy also applied to God, as in Isaiah's prophecy God announces his hope that the remnant of Israel, those who would remain faithful to him, would become the "pride and the glory" of the land. "In that day," God announces through Isaiah in the fourth chapter of his prophecy, "the Branch of the LORD will be beautiful and glorious, and the fruit of the land will be the pride and glory of the survivors of Israel." Clearly, this prophecy applies to the Messiah and also to those faithful souls the Messiah's ministry will produce.

In this Advent season we prepare ourselves for "that day," as Isaiah puts it, the day when we believe God's Messiah came into this world in the person of Jesus. But that preparation involves making sure that the "fruit of our land" points others to the salvation Jesus came to bring. Only then will God's redemptive purposes continue to be advanced generation after generation and the cause of Christ proclaimed to the ends of the earth.

Think about how you might engage in a form of witness that might make that hope more of a reality in the places God puts you today. If so, then God will be pleased with the fruit you produce and in his eyes you too can become God's pride and glory.

How Have We Wearied God?

Malachi 2:17

You have wearied the LORD with your words. "How have we wearied him?" you ask. By saying, "All who do evil are good in the eyes of the LORD, and he is pleased with them" or "Where is the God of justice?"

We all tend to get weary of waiting. Truth be told, I don't know of anyone who enjoys standing in line waiting for the next clerk, sitting in a waiting room listening for his name to be called, or stuck in traffic, anxious for the bottleneck to clear up. Yet in this season of the year we seem to be faced with more waiting than at most other times. And it wearies us.

But have we ever thought about how our waiting wearies God? Or better, I should say how not just the fact of our waiting but the manner in which we wait?

The prophet Malachi is a go-to prophet in our Advent readings because of how Malachi, at the end of our Old Testament, concludes his prophecy with an emphasis on God's messenger, the one who will prepare the way for God's Messiah. In fact, the name Malachi means "My messenger."

In his prophecy Malachi chides the people for how in their impatience for the Messiah to appear they had begun questioning God's justice because of how they had seen so many evil people around them prospering. In other words, if God wills and works for good, then why does God not show up and act when people get away with doing evil? It's a question people still ask today.

God's response, through Malachi, was that in his time God would show up to deal a mortal blow to evil and injustice, and would send a forerunner to make sure his people would be dutifully prepared so they would not miss it. Malachi was to be that messenger in his day, and later John the Baptist would function in that role as a forerunner for Jesus.

Who will be such a messenger in our day? Why not you? At a time when people are impatient for God to show up and act to put this world to rights, why don't you act as that messenger? Through your words and deeds, remind people that our God is an "on time" God; that in the fullness of God's time—at the right moment—God draws near to do for us what we cannot do for ourselves. What they will come to discover is what we have seen in our own lives: When God does show up, as he did in Jesus, the Bethlehem baby, it is always more than worth the wait.

Reaping and Returning with Full Joy

Psalm 126:3-6

The LORD has done great things for us, and we are filled with joy.
Restore our fortunes, LORD, like streams in the Negev.
Those who sow with tears will reap with songs of joy.
Those who go out weeping, carrying seed to sow,
will return with songs of joy, carrying sheaves with them.

On the third Sunday of Advent we light the candle of joy. As you know, joy is very different from happiness. Happiness depends on circumstances working out in our favor. No one is happy when things take a turn for the worst. But joy transcends the circumstances. Even when things take a turn for the worst, what caused that to happen cannot take away our joy.

That's why throughout the Bible we see people of faith locating their joy in a God who transcends life's circumstances. In Psalm 126, the writer invites the people to join him in praising a God who draws near to the captives to deliver them and is capable of changing their circumstances by doing great things that fill them with joy.

In the Christmas season we're reminded of how God did that in sending an angel to announce to the shepherds of Bethlehem that God had for them glad tidings of great joy that should be to all people. Even at a time when Rome had its foot on the throats of Judea's inhabitants, God sent into this world a Savior who would be Christ the LORD. Caesar would not carry the day; Jesus would. Even in those challenging days, people of faith could know God's immeasurable joy.

Nothing has changed as to God's purposes. Oh, we find ourselves facing more than our share of struggles and challenges, trials and tribulations. Maybe that's where some of you are today. But those things don't have to rob you of your joy. God is greater than your trouble. And when you trust him in the midst of it, you will begin to see glimpses of the great things God has in store for you through your faith in Jesus. You will then most certainly be filled with joy.

Surrounded Now and Forevermore

Psalm 125:2

As the mountains surround Jerusalem,
so the LORD surrounds his people both now and forevermore.

It's about this time of the year when we start to hear more talk about the importance of emphasizing "the reason for the season." I'm all about emphasizing the real meaning of Christmas. I get just as bothered as you do over the crass commercialism that has made Christmas into a marketing moment more than the time of holy visitation it was always meant to be.

But that violation of the true meaning of Christmas has been going on for as long as I can remember, and nothing ever seems to change it, not even a pandemic. We just move our shopping from in-person to online. Otherwise, everything is just as profit-driven as it ever was.

So, how might we recover the true meaning of Christmas? It begins with a decision on our part to keep the commercial aspects of the holiday in check. It begins with an acknowledgement that at Christmas God came down to be with us in the person of Jesus so that we wouldn't have to face life's challenges on our own. It begins with the recognition that all of God's redemptive purposes came to fulfillment with the birth of the Bethlehem baby.

One of those promises is recorded in Psalm 125, where the writer points to the hope of God's people that "as the mountains surround Jerusalem, so the LORD surrounds his people, both now and forevermore." It seemed to them that too often when they looked around, they could only see enemies. They could only see nations who were a constant source of threat to their well-being. But the Psalmist invited them to join him in praising the God who in their hour of need would draw near to them to surround them with his mercy and grace.

Today, too many people look around and see a different sort of enemy that threatens our joy, an invisible virus whose specter haunts us at every turn—endangering livelihoods, posing a menace to our health, and bullying us into isolation. It's a tough time. But the good news of Christmas is that God has drawn near to surround us with his presence and every measure of provision we need for the living of such a day. Nothing about COVID will ever call the true meaning of Christmas into question. God's good in Jesus Christ will always prevail, and God's redemption in Jesus will ultimately prevail, today and every day.

Prepare for the Times of Refreshing

Acts 3:19-20

Repent, then, and turn to God, so that your sins may be wiped out,
that times of refreshing may come from the LORD,
and that he may send the Messiah, who has been appointed for you—even Jesus.

As with many of you, I didn't grow up in a church that observed the season of Advent. It wasn't until I was in seminary that I became aware of that part of the Christian tradition and its importance in helping us believers ready ourselves for the Christmas celebration.

One of the things I learned about Advent is that it functions as a "little Lent." Now, growing up I did know a bit about the season of Lent prior to Easter. I knew that it was a time of preparation, reflection, and repentance. But I had never imagined how Advent might also serve such a purpose.

While there is nothing in Scripture about the season of Advent, there is plenty about preparation, reflection, and repentance—and especially how those spiritual practices pertain to Jesus the Messiah. For example, in the book of Acts, as those first believers move out from Jerusalem to fulfill Jesus' great commission, their preaching gives much attention to the importance of turning to the God who has turned to us in his son, our Savior, the LORD Jesus Christ.

In Acts 3, not long after the day of Pentecost, as Simon Peter addresses the crowd that has come together in the temple, he first chides them for their refusal to embrace how God had fulfilled his redemptive promises in the person of Jesus. Peter then invites them to turn from their foolishness by repenting of their ignorance so that they might be forgiven of their sins and made ready for what he calls "the times of refreshing" God has made possible in Jesus Christ.

I like that phrase, "times of refreshing." In fact, I can't think of anything people could benefit from more than "refreshing.".. And you probably share that sentiment. This present season of COVID has been one draining moment after another.

So, let us exercise the gift of Advent and turn from whatever stupor, self-centeredness, and anything else that has left us less aware of the marvelous salvation God has made possible through Jesus Christ. Let us confess and repent, so that even in these stressful times we might know God's seasons of refreshing and be ready when Christmas comes to receive Jesus afresh and anew and the restoration our doing so will bring about.

A Love That Stands Firm Forever

Psalm 89:2

I will declare that your love stands firm forever,
that you have established your faithfulness in heaven itself.

On the last Sunday of Advent we light the candle of love. Of all the aspects of Advent this season represents, I don't know of one that touches us more deeply than the aspect of love. What was it that Bennet Cerf, the great writer of the last century, used to say? "The greatest need any of us has is the need to be loved." That is so true. If we know that we are loved, we can pretty much withstand anything.

Well, the good news of Christmas is that God so loved the world that he gave his only begotten Son. At Christmas God came down to be with us in the Bethlehem baby as the supreme act of his love for us.

God's love is a theme throughout Scripture and is always represented as a firm foundation upon which we can build our lives. In Psalm 89 we are told to declare that God's love stands firm forever. Just when we think there's nothing in life that we can count on because of how everything seems to be in a state of flux, the Psalmist reminds us that we can depend on God's love, which established everything in the very beginning. This world is built on, sustained by, and will culminate in God's love. And at the center of it all, is God's loving act in Bethlehem years ago: the birth of our Savior, Christ the LORD.

Today, you'll have a chance to declare God's firm love, and it may be that God's Spirit will cause you to cross paths with someone in need of it. May you get caught up in the spirit of the Christmas season, which is ultimately love, so that as you give witness to the difference Jesus is making in your life, those persons will see more clearly the answer to their soul's deep longing, God's love in Christ—a firm love, unshakeable and secure to the end.

Fear Not

Luke 2:9-11

Then an angel of the LORD stood before them, and the glory of the LORD shone around them, and they were terrified. But the angel said to them, "Do not be afraid; for see--I am bringing you good news of great joy for all the people: to you is born this day in the city of David a Savior, who is the Messiah, the LORD."

I've always been taken by the number of times in Scripture where an ordinary soul is told to "fear not." I like that King James language. It seems to have more of a sense of punch than some of the modern translations that tell us "not to be afraid." Sometimes when people tell you not to be afraid, you get the feeling that they aren't taking you seriously; that they're not acknowledging the depth of your fear. But when you hear the words, "Fear not," it's almost as if, "Finally, someone understands me." And by acknowledging your fear, their instruction helps you find your faith to move forward.

On this Christmas Eve day a passage of Scripture that will be read in churches and homes around the world is that great text from Luke 2, where the angel of the LORD appears to the shepherds of Bethlehem to tell them of the birth of Jesus, the Messiah.

Of all the wonderful truths in the text, I'm struck by the angel's instruction: "Fear not, for behold, I bring you glad tidings of great joy, which shall be to all people. For unto you is born this day in the city of David, a Savior, which is Christ the LORD." The angel was instructing the shepherds to take their gaze away from all of the uncertainty that had come with his appearance and to turn it instead upon Jesus. In other words, the "behold" is the way to live into the "fear not."

Even on Christmas Eve it's easy to let our attention drift to those things that make us most anxious, that cause us to be uncertain, that make us afraid. But on this day, and for that matter every day, it's better to behold—to behold the gift God sent in the person of Jesus, born in a manger, born to save us from our sins, born to give us the courage and strength for the living of our days. Focus on him and you will never have to be afraid.

Lent

Today Is the Day of Your Salvation
2 Corinthians 6:2

For he says, "At an acceptable time I have listened to you,
and on a day of salvation I have helped you."
See, now is the acceptable time; see, now is the day of salvation!

Today is Ash Wednesday on the Christian calendar. Now, I recognize how for many of you an observance of Ash Wednesday may not have been a part of your faith upbringing, or even if it was, you may have not fully understood its significance. Ask most Christians to define Ash Wednesday and they'll answer that it involves giving up some preference or enjoyment for the 40 days leading up to Easter. But they may not be able to tell you why that act of surrender is so important. As with many aspects of religious observances, we've focused on the peripheral at the expense of the central.

Ash Wednesday has more to do with a prolonged period of preparation for Easter than anything else. Yes, a good bit of that preparation involves surrender and self-denial. But even then, what we may choose to give up is a pledge on our part to gear up for what lies ahead, which is of course the new life God has promised us through our faith in the Risen Christ.

In 2 Corinthians, Paul has spoken with the church about the new creation resurrection faith makes possible. And in chapter 6, as Paul quotes from the Psalmist regarding God's promise to help God's people in the coming day of salvation, Paul boldly and enthusiastically proclaims: "I tell you, now is the time of God's favor, now is the day of salvation." Because Jesus is indeed risen, every day becomes an opportunity for us to experience the new creation that faith in him brings about.

So, even on this Ash Wednesday as we look inwardly and recognize those things we should be giving up, and giving them up for good and not just 40 days, let us also give consideration to what we stand to gain in the process, which is the assurance of Jesus' gracious presence and the ongoing changes he makes possible in us. It may be then that we see whatever we give up, today or any day, pales in comparison to what Jesus provides once we create enough space for him to abide with us.

Walk in the Light

1 John 1:6-7

If we claim to have fellowship with him and yet walk in the darkness, we lie and do not live out the truth. But if we walk in the light, as he is in the light, we have fellowship with one another, and the blood of Jesus, his Son, purifies us from all sin.

You couldn't find a greater contrast in the Bible than the contrast between light and darkness. It shows up in the very first chapter of the first book of the Bible, as the way of describing the orderly and purposeful act of creation God brought about. The Spirit of God hovered over the deep, formless darkness and said, "Let there be light," and thus the story of God's good purposes for our world began.

We see the contrast also in the gospel of John, where speaking of God's Incarnation in Jesus Christ, we are told how "in him was light, and that light was the light of men, and the light shines in the darkness, and the darkness has not overcome it."

We see it again in the first epistle of John, where the progression of light overcoming darkness extends to us, God's being redeemed people, as John warns us not to claim that we belong to God while walking in the darkness at the same time. Our calling is to walk in the light as Jesus is in the light so that we might have fellowship with one another and the blood of Jesus might purify us from all our sins.

In this season of Lent, we understand the importance of being honest with ourselves about our need for the purification that faith in Jesus can bring about. It's not a matter of being honest with God. God understands all too well our tendency to gravitate toward the darkness. But the good news is that God is not willing to stand by and let us lose our life in darkness. God has made possible a light-filled existence if we would but simply confess our sins and trust in his merciful provision in Christ Jesus.

Perhaps that's one of the signal truths in the old saying, "Confession is good for the soul." It's good for the soul. It lets the light of Christ in, the light that makes new creation possible in the same way all creation began and allows that light which the darkness will never overcome to flood our hearts and souls and assure us of the victory that faith in Jesus always secures.

Have a Minute?

Make Your Requests to the God of Great Mercy
Daniel 9:18

Give ear, our God, and hear;
open your eyes and see the desolation of the city that bears your Name.
We do not make requests of you because we are righteous,
but because of your great mercy.

Isn't it interesting how some people approach God with a sense of entitlement, as if they're doing God a favor by going to him with their requests, while others are reluctant to approach God because they know in their hearts that they don't deserve God's help in any way? When we look at Scripture, if you had to make a choice between those two options, clearly, you'd choose the latter. You'd need to approach God as an undeserving soul. Nowhere in Scripture is there commendation for folks who may feel that God owes them something or that they have earned God's favor.

That's a truth we see in Daniel's prophecy (ch. 9), where Daniel is in prayer to God for his people. Daniel was in Babylon, the place of exile, and God's people were there with him because of how they had disobeyed God and incurred God's wrath. As Daniel prays, he comes clean as to how undeserving he and all God's people are of God's favor. He cries out: "Give ear, O God, and hear, open your eyes and see the desolation of the city that bears your name. We do not make requests of you because we are righteous but because of your great mercy" (v. 18).

Daniel shows us the perfect middle ground between entitlement and hopelessness. We approach God boldly, but we approach God in the recognition that whatever God does for us in response to our prayers is because of who God is and not because of who we are or what we deserve.

You've probably heard people say that in this life they only want what they deserve. But do you really want that? Do you really want what you deserve? Daniel would say that it's better to want grace, which you do not deserve, but that God lavishly provides because of who he is, how he loves, and what he wills to do in and through us.

So, come boldly to the throne of grace today through your faith in Jesus Christ. Come boldly but honestly and humbly so that you might find God's mercy and grace for your time of need.

Saved by Grace
Ephesians 2:8-9

For it is by grace you have been saved, through faith—
and this is not from yourselves, it is the gift of God
—not by works, so that no one can boast.

What makes our salvation as Christians so remarkable is that, unlike other world religions that require its adherents to do something to earn their salvation, we understand how ours comes to us by grace, which is nothing less than God's free, unmerited favor extended to us who have trusted our way to Jesus. If it weren't for this remarkable gift, we would have to spend our days fretting over whether we'd done enough to deserve it. But because it is truly a gift that God extends to us in response to our faith, we never have to worry about our moral sufficiency. We instead rest secure in God's moral sufficiency and how that sufficiency has been made known through God's Son our Savior, the LORD Jesus Christ.

The Apostle Paul explains all this in his letter to the Ephesians. In chapter 2, Paul goes into great detail about this truly astounding deliverance God brings about in us, not because of who we are but entirely because of who God is. As Paul describes the former plight of the Ephesian believers who were made alive when once they had been dead because of their trespasses and sins, Paul says: "But God, who is rich in mercy, because of his great love with which he loved us…made us alive together with Christ. For it is by grace you have been saved."

Paul wants his readers to know that their salvation doesn't depend on their actions or accomplishments, their emotions or their feelings. They can rest secure in the wondrous changes God has brought about through his grace in Jesus Christ and then live into those changes not in order to be saved but because they have been saved.

And so can you. Today can be an opportunity for you to try not to earn more grace. That's a contradiction. You can't earn grace. But you can live into it and express it and conduct yourself as a "made alive" person who has all the resources of heaven at your disposal.

According to an old acronym, grace is best understood as "**G**od's **r**iches **a**t **C**hrist's **e**xpense." This saying doesn't exhaust the meaning of grace, but it's a good place to begin. So, start there and go where grace leads you. As the great hymn reminds us, it's always grace that has brought us safe to wherever we are, and it is grace that will lead us home.

Turn Your Ear to the Truth

1 Timothy 4:3-4

For the time will come when people will not put up with sound doctrine. Instead, to suit their own desires, they will gather around them a great number of teachers to say what their itching ears want to hear. They will turn their ears away from the truth and turn aside to myths.

Some people would contend that the day in which we're living is one awash in relativity. It's a day where people make up their own truth and go by their own view of what is right. They say that what is true for you may not be true for me. So, it's just best that we each follow our heart and let our hearts take us where they will.

According to the Bible, we can't trust our hearts. Jeremiah put it this way: "The heart is deceitful above all things, and desperately wicked. Who can know it?" (Jer. 17:9). Because each of us is a sinner, we cannot trust our hearts to take us in a good direction. Truth be told, most of the time they will run us in the ditch. And yet, we find it hard to resist the heart's pull.

In his first letter to Timothy, Paul talked about how such a reality would be a characteristic of the last days, a time when "people will not put up with sound doctrine, but to suit their own desires will gather around them a great number of teachers who will say what their itching ears want to hear." According to Paul, the reason our ears itch so much is because our heart seeks to have its own way.

How then do we resist such temptation? We give our hearts to God's truth. If the heart is deceitful and desperately wicked, then we yield it to God's truth in Jesus, who was the Word, the Truth, and the Life. And as we do so continually, a "wonderful change" takes place within us once Jesus comes into our hearts.

During this season prior to Easter, take the time to open your heart to God's truth. It may not be exactly what you want to hear because it will at some point compel you to deny yourself, take up your cross, and follow Jesus. But when you finally yield your heart to Jesus, you will know everything you need to know; and the changes such knowledge will bring about will do you so very good.

Trust Your Doubts to God

Psalm 77:7-9

Will the LORD reject forever?
Will he never show his favor again?
Has his unfailing love vanished forever?
Has his promise failed for all time?
Has God forgotten to be merciful?
Has he in anger withheld his compassion?

The poet Alfred LORD Tennyson wrote, "There is far more faith in honest doubt than in all the creeds that have ever been written." What Tennyson meant by that sentence is that being honest with our doubts often lands us in a position where our doubts get answered and our faith gets strengthened. Doubt, as it were, exercises faith's muscles; and without doubt, faith would become flabby and weak.

While some people would say that doubt is never a good thing, the Psalmist would side with Tennyson. For example, in Psalm 77, he raises a series of questions, each of which is designed to come clean about his reservations regarding faith in God. Because the Psalmist is in a place where life has taken a turn for the worse, he wonders how long this difficult time will last. He wonders if God has forgotten him. He wonders if he has done something to anger God. "Will the LORD reject forever? Will he never show his favor again?"

Most of us go through such times, and we feel terrible when we do. We feel as if our faith is weak and frail. But what if we were instead to see such doubts as our way of looking to God to provide answers that our minds could never reach? What if we were to see them as our way of going out on a limb that, if it were to break, we would trust God to catch us and keep us safe?

This season prior to Easter is a time for confession. Most of the time we think of confession as involving acknowledgment of our sins. Certainly, confession of sin is appropriate and necessary. But perhaps this time can also be one of confessing our need for God, our dependence upon him and the hope that we have in him. God wants us to be this open and forthright so that he might then draw near and answer our questions, settle our doubts, and secure our eternity through his gift of Christ Jesus.

There is truly more faith in honest doubt than in all the creeds that have ever been written. Doubt takes belief from a sterile page and places it in the nitty-gritty details of everyday life; in the blood, sweat, and tears that not only do we suffer but that Jesus suffered too and Jesus suffered for us. Today, take your doubts to the cross and leave them there. Your faith will become stronger, deeper, and never failing.

Justified by Faith, Not Works

Romans 3:28

For we maintain that a person is justified by faith
apart from the works of the law.

Imagine yourself on trial for a crime that in your heart you know you committed. The case has been argued. The evidence has been presented. Now is the time for the verdict to be given. You know you are guilty, and you have prepared yourself to pay the price for your transgression.

But to your astonishment, when the verdict is read, the decision is "not guilty." You know in your heart you committed the crime. But now you've been spared from having the price. It seems, even in your imagination, too good to be true.

In a nutshell, that's what the gospel is: it's news that seems too good to be true. Though sinners who deserve God's condemnation, through God's gift of Jesus Christ, we have the possibility of being found not guilty, if only we will trust ourselves to Christ and pledge to show faithfulness to all he's done on our behalf.

Such is what the Apostle Paul meant when in Romans 3 he spells out the meaning of justification by faith. The word justification literally comes from the courtroom of Paul's day and refers to one's legal standing as being found "not guilty." But in terms of our salvation, as Paul acknowledges, we've "all sinned and come short of the glory of God." However, Paul assures the Roman Christians that "we maintain that a person is justified by faith apart from the law (v. 28). In other words, it's not what one does to be counted as innocent in God's sight; it's what God has done for us in Christ Jesus and our willingness to trust ourselves to that wondrous gift.

In this season of Lent, we look inwardly to recognize the hopelessness of any effort to earn one's salvation. We acknowledge our sin and our inability to rescue ourselves. We do so not to become discouraged; we do it to think more deeply about grace. And as we do, our faith is strengthened and our hearts rejoice over how through sinners in God's sight we can become saints.

So, today, confess your sins and celebrate your hope in Christ. Turn in faith to him and prepare yourself for the most astounding words of all: "You're not guilty. You're innocent. You're saved by grace and justified by faith. Your faith has made you whole. You can go your way and not be bound by your sin anymore."

Faith Is Credited as Righteousness

Romans 4:4-5

Now to the one who works, wages are not credited as a gift but as an obligation. However, to the one who does not work but trusts God who justifies the ungodly, their faith is credited as righteousness.

Any accountant worth his or her salt will tell you credits are always better than debits. A credit is a positive gain; a debit is an obligation and potentially a burden. To make the ends meet in everyday life, you'd better find a way to secure more credits than debits, more assets than liabilities.

So, how is the balance sheet of your soul these days? That's the ongoing question we are to ask ourselves as we move along in our Lenten journey. How am I doing in terms of growing in God's grace, and are there things in my life that are preventing me from storing up grace's riches?

In his letter to the Romans, Paul talks about how we can make sure that our spiritual balance sheet remains in the black. In the fourth chapter as Paul recounts the story of Abraham, patriarch of the Jews, he emphasizes that Abraham became a model believer because of the manner in which he believed God's promise, even when there was no reason to do so. Of Abraham, Paul says that he believed God and God credited it to him as righteousness. Paul then goes on to speak about how the same thing happens when you and I trust God—God credits our faith as righteousness too.

Working toward our salvation won't get us to where we want to go. In fact, it piles up more spiritual debt upon the existing debt we've accumulated. Our only hope is to trust in what God has done through Jesus to pay all of that spiritual debt and to wipe the slate clean. Only then do we find ourselves celebrating our freedom in Christ and living with an abundance that we could never have found or attained on our own.

It's like an old deacon once prayed during his offertory prayer: "We're living in the red, LORD; we're living in the red." On our own, we certainly are. But when we trust in God's grace in Jesus Christ, the red becomes black, because of the crimson stain that washed all our sins away.

Dare to Believe in God's Blessing

2 Kings 4:16

"About this time next year," Elisha said, "you will hold a son in your arms."
"No, my LORD!" she objected.
"Please, man of God, don't mislead your servant!"

"Things are going so well for me lately I sometimes have to pinch myself to make sure I'm not dreaming." Have you ever heard someone say that? The season of life they are in finds them in such a good place that they hardly can believe their luck. But the sad reality is that not everyone can make such a statement because luck comes and luck goes. Some people would even go so far as to say that "if it weren't for bad luck, I'd have no luck at all."

For people of faith, we don't base our future on luck; we base it on providence, which is nothing less than God's gracious provisions that are based on who God is and not at all on who we are. Because those provisions are based on God's nature, we can be certain that in the long run they will bring us a measure of favor that luck by itself could never bring about. The best news of all is that you don't have to pinch yourself to be alive to it. You just trust it and receive it.

In 2 Kings 4, we're told the gripping story of the Shunammite woman who felt moved to host Elisha. The prophet had been so encouraged by her hospitality that he asked his servant Gehazi how he might show his gratitude. When the servant made his master aware that the woman had no son and that her husband was old, a tragic reality in the ancient world, Elisha called her and informed her that around the same time the following year, she would be holding a son in her arms. The woman's response is poignant and pitiful: "Please, my LORD, do not mislead your servant, O man of God."

The Shunammite woman thought the prophet's blessing was too good to be true. But, of course, it wasn't. And in due time she gave birth to a son. And if you read the rest of the story, even when it seemed that she would lose her son, in God's providence, Elisha made sure that she wouldn't, because God's blessings hold fast to the end.

Maybe some divine favor has come your way and you're worried that it might go as quickly as it came. It won't; and even if it does, something better will follow. And if nothing has come to you despite your devotion to God, keep trusting, because in God's time it will. When it does, it will be as Paul described God's doings to the Ephesians "immeasurably more than we might ask or imagine." Because that's who God is, and that's how God does. God never misleads nor disappoints.

Sustaining the Joy

Genesis 21:6-7

Sarah said, "God has brought me laughter, and everyone who hears about this will laugh with me." And she added, "Who would have said to Abraham that Sarah would nurse children? Yet I have borne him a son in his old age."

A challenge we each face with our faith is finding a way to maintain our sense of joy. Part of that is because our attention gets redirected from the favor God has bestowed upon us in days past due to the challenges we must contend with in the present day. Sadly, the challenges always seem to find a way to cancel out the favor. But one way to keep life's challenges from robbing us of our joy is to look for ways to keep God's joy ever before us.

By definition, joy isn't dependent on situations or circumstances. Therefore, if we can think about how to sustain our memories of God's joy, then no matter how dismal the circumstances become, we will not have to forfeit our joy in the face of them.

I like what Sarah did in the book of Genesis. When her husband Abraham was visited by the LORD in the form of three men, as they were sharing God's promise to bring Abraham and Sarah a son in their old age, Sarah was eavesdropping on their conversation and upon hearing God's promise laughed to herself at the thought of such favor. When confronted with her response, Sarah lied. It was simply too good to be true.

But the thing about God's favor is that it's always too good to be true. So, according to Genesis 21, Sarah gives birth to the son of promise, she decides to name the child Isaac, which means laughter. Her explanation says it all: "God has brought me laughter, and everyone who hears about this will laugh with me." Isaac's name would be an ongoing reminder to Sarah and to Abraham and to everyone else in their social network that God's promise always results in joy.

Maybe today you're in a place where you are on the verge of losing your sense of joy. Think carefully about the last promise God brought about for you, and hold on to it. Name it. Claim it. Sustain it. Keep it ever before you. Bear witness to it so that others might help keep you accountable to it. Then no matter how difficult the trials and tribulations and temptations of life become, you won't lose your joy. You've aligned your life around it. It will always be news that is too good to be true. But if God has made it become reality, then you can be certain its joy—God's joy—will abide with you every day in every way.

Where Is the Lamb?

Genesis 21:6-8

Abraham took the wood for the burnt offering and placed it on his son Isaac, and he himself carried the fire and the knife. As the two of them went on together, Isaac spoke up and said to his father Abraham, "Father?" "Yes, my son?" Abraham replied. "The fire and wood are here," Isaac said, "but where is the lamb for the burnt offering?" Abraham answered, "God himself will provide the lamb for the burnt offering, my son." And the two of them went on together.

The story in Genesis 22 of Abraham's willingness to sacrifice his son Isaac on Mount Moriah at God's command is one of the most poignant stories in the Bible. It is also one of the more perplexing. The story is poignant in how it represents the depth of Abraham's faith.

Isaac was the child of promise, the son Abraham and Sarah never thought they would have. So, when the command of God was to offer him up in the same way that Abraham's pagan neighbors sacrificed their children, it seems remarkable that Abraham would have been willing to do so—no questions asked. I'm especially gripped by the part where, as Isaac realizes how they have everything they need for the sacrifice but the lamb, he asks what he most likely already knows to be the answer to the question "Where is the lamb?" Abraham answers "God will provide." That part tears my heart out every time I read it.

But, of course, there's the perplexing part to the story: We have questions: Why would God have asked such a thing from Abraham? What kind of God would put someone through such a test and ask him to make such a sacrifice? The only answer is: a God who would be willing to sacrifice his own son for us and our salvation.

As poignant as Abraham's story is, it makes no good sense without reading it in the shadow of the cross. On Moriah, God saw Abraham's faith, rejoiced in it, and did not ask Abraham to go through with his sacrifice of his son. God provided another lamb. But at Calvary, God showed his faith to his redemptive promises by allowing his Son, our Savior, to die for us sinners. Now, we're back to the poignancy. "Greater love hath no man than this: that a man lay down his life for his friends." And a greater love God could never show, for he has so loved this world that he gave his only begotten son.

I don't know what God may be calling you to sacrifice today. But I do know that it won't rise to the level of what he asked of Abraham, simply because in Jesus God has already done all the sacrificing necessary. No, actually that's not true. There is a sacrifice you will be called to give—the sacrifice of your own life, the yielding of your own will and desires so that God's new life in Jesus Christ might be found.

So, remember the poignancy of God's love expressed in Christ Jesus. Let that demonstration of love answer all the other perplexities that might be in your heart. Where is the Lamb? He is on the cross. Deny yourself, take up your cross, and follow after him so that you might know the abundant life that faith in Jesus always brings—now and forevermore.

Love No Praise More than God's

John 12:42-43

Yet at the same time many even among the leaders believed in him. But because of the Pharisees they would not openly acknowledge their faith for fear they would be put out of the synagogue; for they loved human praise more than praise from God.

It seems now that every decision gets made on the basis of what the polls say. Public opinion has become the final arbiter on pretty much everything in life. I understand that in part. As a leader, if you turn around and you don't have anyone following you, you only are taking a walk. But on the other hand, if you let the crowd lead and you base your decisions only so that you can avoid losing favorability with the masses, you've forfeited your responsibility and you've succumbed to public opinion. That's true not only for leaders, but also for followers. You're better basing your decisions on your core values and not the whims of others.

We see this danger in John 12, where Jesus has entered into Jerusalem to fulfill God's mission by going to the cross. (Talk about thumbing your nose at public opinion!) Jesus' willingness to embrace the shame and ignominy of Calvary shows just how much he is connected to the Father. Jesus is reflecting on the refusal of the religious leaders to receive him, in spite of the miraculous signs they have seen him perform. John states the reason for the lack of their acceptance: "they loved praise from men more than praise from God."

Salvation is not a popularity contest. It's not a way to get ahead in the world. It won't always win you friends or help you influence people. But it will give you life and give it to you in abundance.

So, today, I'm not asking you to turn people off intentionally. I'm only asking you to follow Jesus and let the chips fall where they may. If you do, God will praise you and reward you and give you life, even as he did Jesus by raising him from the dead. God will give you everlasting life through your belief in Jesus, life now and life forevermore.

Called Out of Darkness Into Marvelous Light

1 Peter 2:9-10

But you are a chosen people, a royal priesthood, a holy nation, God's special posses-
sion, that you may declare the praises of him who called you out of darkness into his
wonderful light. Once you were not a people, but now you are the people of God; once
you had not received mercy, but now you have received mercy.

The time change is drawing near, for which I always am a bit ambivalent. On the one hand,
I don't like losing the hour of sleep on that first Sunday of the time change, especially when
I have to gear up an hour earlier to preach a sermon. That one day usually requires a couple
of weeks for my biological clock to get reset. But on the other hand, I love having the extra
daylight in the afternoon; as a golfer, it allows for a quick nine holes or a little bit of practice
time once I leave the office. So, when I weigh the upside and the downside of the springing
forward, it's the extra hour of daylight that always wins.

From what I can gather from others, most folks feel the same way. They like the extra
sunshine. Even if you don't like being outdoors, there's something about the light that lifts
your spirits and settles your soul.

That's also a spiritual truth according to Scripture. In Peter's first letter, where he writes
to new Christians about what it means to be a redeemed people, he impresses upon them
how they are chosen and holy and a people belonging to God. In the second chapter he uses
a phrase that I hope would resonate with all of us today. God has done all of this through
Jesus Christ so that "you may declare the praises of him who called you out of darkness
into his wonderful light" (v. 9). Of course, the darkness was that of our sins, a darkness
that clouded our way and obstructed our path. But with God's light, the light of his salvation in Christ Jesus, we know that our future is full of hope and our way into it will be
unobstructed.

In this season of Lent, that's the journey we are invited to make. And like the calendar
time change that finds us so tired of the darkness that we are ready for some light, so does
our faith journey point us in the direction of celebrating the added purpose that life in
Christ always makes possible.

As the time change approaches, I hope that you're getting excited about getting more
sunlight at your disposal. And I also hope that even though Easter is still some weeks away,
you're using this time to prepare yourself for the glorious light of resurrection morning that
our faith in Jesus allows us to know.

Even if today seems dismal, remember how it always does seem darkest before the
dawn. And God's calling is ultimately to an unending and eternal light, one that the
darkness will never overcome.

Refresh Your Soul

Psalm 18:7

The law of the LORD is perfect,
refreshing the soul.

I've always been intrigued at how words get repackaged so that their meanings reflect new realities. For example, the word "refresh." At one time the word suggested a renewal of spirit, but now when your internet goes down or your computer signal gets messed up, you speak about needing to refresh things in order to get them back to working order.

Truth be told, I like the old definition a lot better. I like to think about refreshment more along personal lines than technical ones. I like contemplating the possibilities of being renewed and reenergized and reinvigorated for the challenges that lie before me.

That's why this season before Easter is so important. It's not just a time for reflection and remorse. Those emotions are not the end; they are a means to a higher end, a more refreshing end. The purpose of our reflection and repentance is to help us get to a place where our souls are restored to working order and our hearts are reenergized to the tasks at hand.

In Psalm 19 there's this wonderful litany as to how the law of God is perfect because "it refreshes the soul." It's the Psalmist's way of saying that far from being burdensome, God's expectations for us his people are ones that are life-giving. I love the Psalmist's description of them: They're trustworthy. They are right. They give joy and light. They are pure and endure forever. Just hearing these promises allows the refreshing breeze of God's Spirit to awaken hopes and dreams we may have thought life might have dashed forever.

So, today, consider ordering your life around God's expectations. Reflect on the possibilities and repent of anything that might keep you from them. After all, how much better can you get than perfect, and how much more uplifting than that which revives?

From Strength to Strength

Psalm 84:5-7

Blessed are those whose strength is in you, whose hearts are set on pilgrimage. As they pass through the Valley of Baka, they make it a place of springs; the autumn rains also cover it with pools. They go from strength to strength, till each appears before God in Zion.

The fitness industry is as big a business today as any other. Granted, there have always been people who have done their best to stay in shape or even get in better shape. But nowadays it seems as if every age and every activity has a fitness regimen designed to help you live with optimum vigor and energy.

So, how is your spiritual stamina these days? That's a question we ought to ask ourselves from time to time, especially during those seasons when we find ourselves facing challenges that tend to sap our strength. In those times we need to make sure that we are connected to a source of inexhaustible spiritual vitality that will keep us going come what may.

In Psalm 84 there is a wonderful expression the Psalmist employs as he describes the benefits of placing one's trust in God. He tells us that for those who are "strong in the LORD" they go "from strength to strength." I love that expression. They don't go from strength to exhaustion or even from strength to "let's take a rest for a moment." They go instead from strength to strength. And it's not that they never encounter setbacks along the way. They often must go through "the Valley of Baka," which can also be translated the Valley of Weeping. Yet even then that valley becomes a place of refreshing springs as God's people make their way to the good place God is calling them to be.

It may be that today you're in a place of weeping, a tough place, a draining place. It's often the case that we have to go through those places in order to grow strong in God. More than likely, it's so that we can understand the importance of leaning upon God's strength and not our own.

So, even in the midst of whatever challenge has come your way, see it as an opportunity to lean more fully upon God's strength so that you may learn more fully of God's faithfulness. Then you will be strong in the LORD and whatever path you find yourself on will be one that will eventually lead you to where God is so that you arrive in his presence stronger and better for your journey.

Yearn to Be in the Presence of God

Psalm 84:1-2

How lovely is your dwelling place, LORD Almighty!
My soul yearns, even faints, for the courts of the LORD;
my heart and my flesh cry out for the living God.

Most of us are accustomed to going where we want to go and when. But when the Covid-19 pandemic hit, our schedules got interrupted and we were forced to stay away from restaurants and movie theaters and sports events and family gatherings and even church. Fortunately, as things improved, we were able to participate in more of those types of activities, and now with the availability of three vaccines we can see light at the end of what has been an exceedingly long and dark tunnel.

In Psalm 84 the writer gives expression to how he yearns, even faints, for the opportunity to go into the courts of the LORD. That phrase "courts of the LORD" refers of course to the temple complex, where God's people would gather to give thanks to God for his manifold blessing. It was in the temple that the Psalmist felt most at home, and as we read the psalm many of us can appreciate the angst expressed in it when someone is kept from being with others in worshiping God in spirit and in truth.

The good news of this season is that God has drawn near to us wherever we may be, and God has drawn near to do for us what he alone can do. And so, it may be that church is not yet on the list of places you feel it is safe to go. Staying away from the house of God temporarily does not mean that you have to forfeit finding rest in God's presence. God is right there where you are, even today, and nothing will ever separate you from his love in Christ Jesus.

So, in due time, you'll be able to return to worship with other brothers and sisters to celebrate the good news of our faith. In the meantime, you can celebrate right where you are. And while you do, the yearning you feel will make the return to worship when it happens even better, as you join with others in crying out for the living God, who in Jesus extends to us life forevermore.

Go Your Way 'Till the End

Daniel 12:13

As for you, go your way till the end.
You will rest, and then at the end of the days
you will rise to receive your allotted inheritance.

There's something about completing a task that always brings joy and fulfillment. Even if it's a hard task, if we can imagine the good that we will feel at the end of it, that image can often sustain us even when we're on the verge of giving up.

Perseverance is an important element to our faith. Throughout Scripture we are told that only those who keep the faith through to the end will know salvation. We are also told that God will gladly provide every resource needed to do so. So, instead of worrying if we can hold out to the end, we would be much better served by trusting in God's help day by day.

In Daniel 12 we read a highly symbolic passage that speaks to the importance of enduring to the end. Daniel knew from personal experience the challenges of holding to one's faith. We may think that being in a lion's den was a piece of cake for him, but reading the entire prophecy helps us to see that Daniel persevered just as any of us is able to do—by trusting the situation to God and asking God for help.

Although Daniel doesn't give a specific date—such as March 12, 2021—he talks about the end times. He talks figuratively of "a time, another two times, and a half a time." These figures come out to three and a half years, a fraction of the perfect number 7. It symbolizes a time that has yet to be completed. Then he goes on to talk about 1,290 days and 1,335 days—which essentially add up to the same amount of time and also suggests incompleteness. But what is crystal clear is verse 13, where Daniel is told by the man in linen, "As for you, go your way till the end." In other words, use this time to prepare yourself for your eternal reward.

All we have is today. We're not guaranteed tomorrow, and we cannot reclaim yesterday. But because our faith assures us that we don't have to be held back by our pasts or uncertain about our future security, we can live every moment with fullness and joy.

Why not make it a point to do that today, trusting when the way becomes difficult to the promise of grace that will enable you to keep going? As Daniel was told, this day may involve some challenge. But at the end you will rest, and will rise to receive your allotted inheritance. Daniel's words remind us of Jesus' promise that "they who persevere to the end will be saved" (Mark 13:13). So trust in Jesus to help you get to the end in grace, and to get there in grace one step at a time until your journey is complete.

Be Careful Not to Fall

1 Corinthians 10:12

So if you think you are standing,
watch out that you do not fall.

There is nothing more embarrassing than to trip, lose your footing, and fall. When we're younger, it's just our pride that gets hurt, but as we age, we can't afford to fall, lest the injury becomes something more serious. But whether young or old, the worst injury from a fall happens when we stumble spiritually. Usually, that happens when we're not paying serious attention to whatever situation has come against us. We think we're capable of meeting it, and we start relying upon our own power instead of God's power through his grace in Jesus Christ.

In Paul's first letter to the church at Corinth, he finds it necessary to admonish believers there who had become too full of themselves. They were thinking themselves to be wiser and stronger and more special than they were. In chapter 10, Paul goes into great detail over how our human desire to be masters of our own destinies goes all the way back to the beginning, which we can see played out in the history of the Israelites wandering in the wilderness on their way to Canaan. Though sustained by God's miraculous provisions, Israel grumbled and complained and whined about wanting to be delivered from their dependence on God. As for the ones who ended up falling into sin, none of them made it into Canaan, the land of promise. So, how does Paul apply that story to the Corinthians? He warns those believers, "If you think you are standing firm, be careful that you don't fall." In other words, recognize how fragile and flimsy everyday life is so that the only way any of us can remain standing is by trusting in what God has done for us in Jesus Christ.

Today may be one of those days when you're feeling pretty steady. I hope it stays that way for you. But as you know, a prop could get knocked out from under you at any moment. Some of you have already had that happen and now you're struggling to get back on your feet. Lean on Jesus and his everlasting arms. You will then be safe and secure from all alarms as you build your life on the strongest of foundations, one that will never give way, one that will withstand the fiercest of storms, one that will be your refuge and your strength.

EASTERTIDE

Shouts of Joy and Victory

Psalm 118:15

Shouts of joy and victory resound in the tents of the righteous:
"The LORD's right hand has done mighty things!"

Watching sporting events over the course of this last year has been an interesting thing for me. For the longest time I had this sensation deep within me that something wasn't right, even though I was grateful for the opportunity to watch something somewhat normal during the time when so many other things had been taken away. The more I thought about it, the more I began to see what seemed "off"—these events were occurring without spectators. There wasn't a crowd on hand to cheer and applaud when their side did something good. The lack of fan participation left something to be desired, so I for one am happy to see them returning to the action, though gradually.

I bring that notion of fan participation up on the day after Easter because of how our response as believers to the good news of resurrection cannot be overlooked or minimized. News such as that which God has made possible in raising Jesus from the dead cannot be silenced. It must be voiced and proclaimed, not that the victory of Jesus over the grave would be endangered by the silence, but that others wouldn't necessarily appreciate the magnitude and magnificence of what Easter is all about.

In Psalm 118, a messianic song, we are told: "Shouts of joy and victory resound in the tents of the righteous: 'The LORD's right hand has done mighty things.'" In other words, it's not that God's work hinges on whether people notice it, but rather that God's work deserves to be trumpeted and applauded and celebrated with the highest expression of joy possible.

For some of us, the day after Easter is something of a downer. It's as if, after all the celebration of yesterday, today things are supposed to go back to normal. But the whole point of Easter is that things can't go back to normal. Things will never go back to normal. There's now a "new" normal. He is still risen, so let us glory in that good news with shouts of joy and victory.

Jesus Goes Ahead of You

Mark 16:6-7

"Don't be alarmed," he said. "You are looking for Jesus the Nazarene, who was cruci-fied. He has risen! He is not here. See the place where they laid him. But go, tell his disciples and Peter, 'He is going ahead of you into Galilee. There you will see him, just as he told you.'"

If you've ever tried to follow someone in a car to an unfamiliar location, you know how hard and how frustrating that is. Of course, nowadays we put our destination in our naviga-tion app, but sometimes someone invites us to follow to make sure that we don't get lost. Even then, the traffic and the stop lights, the twists and the turns often make that effort exasperating and so, more times than not, we say to those persons, "Just go ahead and I'll meet you there."

That image comes to mind when I read the Easter story from Mark's gospel. As in all resurrection stories there is a commission that's a part of it, a word of instruction from God not to keep such glorious news to oneself but to share it with others, especially those who desperately need it. In this case, the angel who appeared to the women on that first Easter morning tells them to go to Jesus' disciples—in particular Simon Peter, who had betrayed Jesus—and instruct them that "he is going before them into Galilee, where you will see him, just as he had told you."

On that first Easter morning, the disciples were not with the women, but were instead still locked away in hiding lest they meet the same fate as their Master. But now they will be told the good news of the gospel—that Jesus has been raised from the dead and is going ahead to meet them in their most familiar place, Galilee, which was their home.

It's been several days since we gathered to celebrate the resurrection story. We've returned to our everyday life, with all the headaches and heartaches that everyday life can bring. But what difference might it make if we knew that wherever this day might take us and whatever headaches and heartaches will be there to meet us, Jesus will be there to meet us also? In the presence of the Risen Jesus all headaches go away and all heartaches are replaced by everlasting joy.

As you go on with your life, be certain that Jesus will be wherever your life takes you. He will be there to strengthen you and to save you. He will be there so that you may know the joy of the salvation his risen presence makes possible and through your embrace of him and his Easter power, your joy will be complete.

Trust God's Provision
Daniel 1:11-14

Daniel then said to the guard whom the chief official had appointed over Daniel, Hananiah, Mishael and Azariah, "Please test your servants for ten days: Give us nothing but vegetables to eat and water to drink. Then compare our appearance with that of the young men who eat the royal food, and treat your servants in accordance with what you see." So he agreed to this and tested them for ten days.

The hardest thing for many of us to believe is that if God calls us to a certain task, God will then provide what is necessary for us to accomplish it. In other words, God's not going to leave us "hanging out to dry." Whatever is required to do God's bidding, God will make sure that we have it in abundance, and even more.

I'm reminded of that truth in the story of Daniel and the three other Jewish youths who were taken into Babylon when Nebuchadnezzar conquered the city. Daniel, Shadrach, Meschach, and Abednego (or Hananiah, Mishael, and Azariah, if you're calling them by their Hebrew names) were pressed into the king's service and ordered to eat from the king's table. But Daniel asked Nebuchadnezzar's servant to let them eat in accordance with God's expectations and to give them 10 days to do so before passing judgment on their request.

The servant agreed to the request, and Daniel and the other three youths were far superior to their Babylonian counterparts. Nebuchadnezzar was so impressed that he put them in places of high authority. But in fact, it was God who wanted them in such a place and was equipping them to stand firm for him so that Nebuchadnezzar and all the Babylonians might see that the God of the youths was the God above all other gods.

Sometimes we roll our eyes when we sense God calling us to a particular task and see what we have on hand to fulfill it. But remember, God makes a habit out of taking the small things and using them to his glory. God has already allowed Jesus to be nailed to the cross so that you don't have to. Indeed, Jesus' sacrifice is all the provision you need; his grace will be sufficient for your every need.

Today, approach the throne of grace boldly so that you may receive God's grace in your time of need. If you do, others will notice it, and will be drawn to the God who has done through you great things. What a difference it makes to know that God gives us all we require to be found faithful so that our lives might teem with abundance, even the abundance that Jesus promised all his disciples would know.

Speak the Word of God Boldly

Acts 4:29-31

"Now, LORD, consider their threats and enable your servants to speak your word with great boldness. Stretch out your hand to heal and perform signs and wonders through the name of your holy servant Jesus." After they prayed, the place where they were meeting was shaken. And they were all filled with the Holy Spirit and spoke the word of God boldly.

If there's anything we need more in the church, it's for believers in Jesus to be bolder in their witness for him. That doesn't mean just talking rashly or impulsively. It means being open to God's spirit so that both our words and our deeds point others to the Risen Christ.

Boldness is one of the key concepts in the book of Acts, which gives an account of the gospel's advance from Jerusalem, to Judea and Samaria, and ultimately to the uttermost parts of the earth. In Acts 4, the day of Pentecost has come and the promised Holy Spirit, that dynamite from above, has fallen upon the believers. Remarkable things are happening, primarily in the way the believers go forth into their world to speak the message of Jesus despite the opposition doing so brings about.

Peter and John have just been let out of prison. They return to where the other believers have gathered, and they praise God together over how God has allowed them to speak his word "with great boldness." But not being satisfied with that anointing, they pray for more opportunities to display God's power in their world, even his power that had raised Jesus from the dead. And as they pray, the room where they have gathered begins shaking, and they are filled with the Holy Spirit and speak the word of God boldly.

The boldness believers need to show today for Jesus only comes through the filling of the Holy Spirit, which is not so much an emotional thing as it is a simple openness on our part for God to speak truth through us, through our words, and through our actions. Today, you'll have the opportunity to stand fast for Jesus in places God sends you, some of which may require your boldness. When you find yourself in such a place, be open to God's presence and then respond as the Spirit leads you. You may be surprised to discover that even that place can become shaken by the Spirit of God as people come to see Easter power in your spirit, Easter power that may lead them to be open to the Spirit of Jesus himself that they too may know the boldness to which all fear will always give way.

Worship God Alone
Daniel 3:16-18

Shadrach, Meshach and Abednego replied to him, "King Nebuchadnezzar, we do not need to defend ourselves before you in this matter. If we are thrown into the blazing furnace, the God we serve is able to deliver us from it, and he will deliver us from Your Majesty's hand. But even if he does not, we want you to know, Your Majesty, that we will not serve your gods or worship the image of gold you have set up."

The first commandment God gave to Moses was that God's people should have no other gods before him. God's people should worship him and him alone. While that commandment may seem to be a simple one to follow, for people in the ancient world it was not. Competing gods were everywhere, and God's people were constantly being required to spurn them—and sometimes at great costs.

Nowhere in Scripture do we see the costs of worshiping God alone more than in the story of Shadrach, Meshach, and Abednego, those three Hebrews young men who had been brought before King Nebuchadnezzar for their unwillingness to bow down before the king's statue. The king challenged them with the ultimatum, "If you don't bow down, I'll cast you into the fiery furnace." I find the young men's response to be remarkable: "We have nothing to talk about with regard to this matter. Our God will deliver us. But if he chooses not to, we'll not bow down anyway." The king made good on his threats and threw them into the fiery furnace. And God made good on his promise to deliver them. They emerged from the furnace completely unscathed.

We may think that the pressure to worship other gods in our day is not very strong. But it's more the case that the gods that vie for our attention and adoration are just more subtle. The pressure is just as great, and the peril for not worshiping them is just as strong. But giving in to the pressure will not bring about joy or peace, and it certainly won't bring about salvation. Only trusting in God as God trusted himself to us in Jesus will get us to where we want to be.

So, today, worship God and God alone. Have no other gods before him. No matter how much the pressure builds or how hot the criticism becomes, God will make for you a way; a way that will see you through to a better time and a better place, one that holds the promise of everything in life you yearn for, and even more.

Do Not Love the World

1 John 2:15-17

Do not love the world or anything in the world. If anyone loves the world, love for the Father is not in them. For everything in the world—the lust of the flesh, the lust of the eyes, and the pride of life—comes not from the Father but from the world. The world and its desires pass away, but whoever does the will of God lives forever.

What is the first Bible verse you memorized? Most people would answer "John 3:16—For God so loved the world that he gave his only begotten son that whosoever believeth in him should not perish but have everlasting life." Well, you might ask, "If God so loved the world, then why does the Bible tell us not to?"

I'm thinking of that teaching in the first epistle of John, the same John who was responsible for that verse you memorized first; the John who, at a later point in his life, told the church: "Do not love the world or anything in the world." How can we reconcile God's love for the world with John's warning for us not to?

The answer lies in making sure that our love and loyalty are in the right order. The problem for most folks is that when they love the world too much, they have no room to love God, which is the point John was making in his epistle. In fact, John goes on to say that if someone loves the world, "the love of God is not in him." He's used up all the space in his heart for the world. God has nothing left to occupy. John would recommend that if we make sure God has enough space in our hearts and that we love him rightly, then all our other loves and loyalties will be expressed from a place that God controls. How did the early theologian Augustine put it? "Love God and do as you please."

Think about that today as you go about your life. Try to see everything in light of God's love for you and your love for him. Allow God's love to flow through you by way of your faith in Jesus Christ so that your entire being will result in worship and praise. After all, what the world needs now is love, sweet love. But it doesn't need your love; it needs God's love. And when you become the instrument through whom God's love pours out, every place you go will be a better place—quite possibly even a holy place.

Kept in Perfect Peace

Isaiah 26:3

You will keep in perfect peace those whose minds are steadfast,
because they trust in you.

In a conflicted world such as ours today, I don't know of anything people are looking for more than a sense of peace. If we could find a way to lower life's temperature of life or even turn down the volume, then we could manage things so much easier. But unfortunately, we can't. Those kinds of things are simply beyond our control.

But they're not beyond God's control. We're reminded of this truth by the prophet Isaiah. The 26th chapter of Isaiah deals with a time in the life of God's people when they were being attacked by the Assyrians, who had overrun the northern kingdom of Israel and were now on the verge of doing the same for the southern kingdom of Judah. As Isaiah sought to encourage the people, he assured them that if they would set their hearts upon God, he would keep them in what Isaiah calls "perfect peace," which can also be translated as "full peace" or "complete peace." God's people would never know such peace in their own power; only those who steadfastly trusted in God would come to experience such remarkable peace.

Interestingly, the word peace does not suggest an absence of conflict, which is how we define peace today. It's more a sense of well-being, an assurance that everything will be OK even when it's not OK at the present moment. The word in Hebrew is *shalom* and while a word of greeting among God's people, it also is a witness to what God alone can do.

This idea shows up in the New Testament, where Jesus is referred to as the Prince of Peace. God could have done nothing greater than what he did in Jesus, who is alive and well today and whose abiding presence makes us fully alive and fully well.

So, in whatever conflict and discord you may be going through today, look for Jesus, who has not forsaken you and never will. Let Jesus connect you to the peace of God "which passes all understanding." Trust your todays and tomorrows to him: he promises to do for you what you could never do for yourself. He will keep you in "perfect peace."

Dwell in God's Safety
Psalm 4:8

In peace I will lie down and sleep,
for you alone, LORD, make me dwell in safety.

Normally, April 15 would be a day few of us would be looking forward to. That's because in most years, it's the last day we have to file our tax return. But this year we've been given a reprieve with COVID, but even then it only prolongs the inevitable.

There are two things in life that are certain, as they say: death and taxes. When you compare those two, maybe taxes aren't such a bad thing after all. Still, between death and taxes, there are lots of other things that cause us distress. And it's not just one day we have to deal with those things; it's every day. So, how do we deal with our anxieties and challenges?

According to Psalm 4, we trust them to God. This psalm is a plea to God to answer the faithful in their distress, and as the Psalmist considers God's faithfulness to do that and more. He concludes the psalm with this statement of assurance and rest: "I will lie down and sleep in peace, for you alone, O LORD, make me dwell in safety." God's presence calms our anxieties, and God's power overcomes all our challenges.

What was the first prayer you learned as a child? My guess is that it might have been: "Now, I lay me down to sleep. I pray the LORD my soul to keep. If I should die before I wake, I pray the LORD my soul to take." And with that prayer, you rested in God, even as a child.

Death and taxes: that's a tough combo. As far as the other stuff in between, it only makes life more unsettling. But pray for the LORD to keep your soul, whether awake or asleep. Then you won't have to worry about anything. God will enable you to dwell in his safety, where all is well. Death won't have the last word: God will. And knowing your life is in God's hands is not taxing at all!

Don't Be Led Astray

1 John 2:26-27

I am writing these things to you about those who are trying to lead you astray. As for you, the anointing you received from him remains in you, and you do not need anyone to teach you. But as his anointing teaches you about all things and as that anointing is real, not counterfeit—just as it has taught you, remain in him.

Whenever you find yourself in a place where you don't know where you're going, you have a choice: You can either hope you find your destination on your own, or you can break down and ask someone for directions. I know as a man how hard it is to admit I'm lost and in need of some help. Truth be told, most of the time I've ended up asking someone who wasn't from around there anyway. He was as clueless as I was. So, it wouldn't have made much sense to listen to anything he might have told me anyway.

Yet, strangely, a lot of people seem to do just that with respect to life. We all are in need of help, but finding the right direction won't come from other people who think they are experts; they are just as lost as we are. The only way to know how to move forward in life and to get to where we want to be is to trust in the direction God has provided in the person of Jesus.

In his first epistle, John writes to a church in need of basic direction. In chapter 2, he warns them not to be led astray by people who are just as in need of help as they. He encourages them instead to trust their way to Jesus and to "the anointing" they have in him. That anointing of course refers to the Holy Spirit, the Counselor and Advocate whom Jesus said would lead us into all truth. Through the Spirit's presence, Jesus abides in us. And by following the Spirit's direction, even as did Jesus, we will never be led astray.

So, if you're feeling a bit lost today, don't trust your way to anyone other than Jesus. He came to seek and save those who are lost and to show them a way to life everlasting. Let Jesus who abides with you keep you on the straight and narrow, the only path that will get us to where we want to be: the place he has prepared for us in God's presence, where we might find everything we're looking for—and more.

Know You Have Passed from Death to Life

1 John 3:14

We know that we have passed from death to life,
because we love each other.

In John 5, Jesus answered criticisms leveled against him not only for performing miracles on the Sabbath but also for explaining how he was following God's direction, a direction that if people believed him would enable them to cross over from death to life. That message obviously sunk in with John because of how in his first epistle he repeats that teaching as he encourages believers to be known for their love for one another. In chapter 3 John assures them, "For we know that we have passed from death to life because we love our brothers and sisters." The love that God had shown in sending his only begotten son into the world to make possible everlasting life always shows up whenever believers display that love in their interactions with one another.

In this Easter season, are you living into that display? As people look at you, do they see how you are wishing for the best and working for the best in others? I understand that some people are not likeable. (We probably aren't likeable to them either, but that's beside the point.) If we can open our hearts to Easter power so that it changes everything about us for the better, then that change will be evidenced through the way we treat one another. If we show love, the emotion may then follow. But don't wait for the emotion to generate the action: you'll be waiting for eternity. Instead, do the deed and trust the feeling to follow. Show your love and then you will be showing that you are an Easter person.

My guess is that we'll all have a chance to put our love on display today. That's how the Spirit works. When your chance comes, remember the love God showed you in sending Jesus to suffer, to die, and to be raised to life for you to have everlasting life. The same power that brought life out of his death can bring love out of your hardened heart and give you the assurance that you're on the right track, the track that leads to abundant life now and everlasting life forevermore.

God's Healing Presence

Hosea 6:1-3

Come, let us return to the LORD. He has torn us to pieces but he will heal us; he has injured us but he will bind up our wounds. After two days he will revive us; on the third day he will restore us, that we may live in his presence. Let us acknowledge the LORD; let us press on to acknowledge him. As surely as the sun rises, he will appear; he will come to us like the winter rains, like the spring rains that water the earth.

None of us enjoys being sick. It matters not what kind of sickness—whether physical, emotional, or spiritual—whenever we're not at our best, we're not fun to be around. When I'm feeling sick, I want to shut the door, crawl in the bed, and be left alone until I get to feeling better. Of course, that works when it comes to physical sickness. But when I'm not feeling my best emotionally or spiritually, I need an outside presence to get me back on track.

God sent the prophet Hosea in the Old Testament to announce healing and restoration to a spiritually sick nation. God had called Hosea to marry a woman of questionable character to show the nation of Israel how they had been unfaithful to God. Then when Hosea's wife ran off, God told Hosea to go out and find her and be reconciled to her as God's way of assuring the people that he would never give up on them.

In Hosea 6 we find these words of God's desire to restore his people: "Come, let us return to the LORD. He will heal us. He will bind up our wounds. After two days he will revive us and on the third day he will restore us that we may live in his presence."

The mention of the third day points to the ultimate healing and restoration God made possible for us by raising Jesus from the dead. The Risen Jesus was torn to pieces on the cross and injured on our behalf as a way of taking upon himself the burden of our sins. On the third day God raised him from the dead as God's way of saying that nothing can ever separate us from his love in Christ Jesus.

Today, you may feel torn and injured, hurt and hopeless. You may feel sick. God can make you well through your faith in Jesus, the Great Physician. Acknowledge him in all you're about and when people today see you and the difference that Jesus is making in you, don't be surprised if they tell you, "You look great! I've never seen you looking better!" And what a great opportunity you will then have to tell them why.

Use Your Breath to Praise the LORD

Psalm 150:6

Let everything that has breath praise the LORD.

Our breath is the best indication that we are alive. That's why when someone is concerned about another person who may be on death's doorstep, the question is often asked, "Is he breathing?" Having no breath is not a good sign!

The notion of breath is of course an important symbol in the Bible of being fully alive. In the book of Genesis, when God creates Adam and breathes into his nostrils "the breath of life," Adam becomes a living soul.

In Psalm 150 the writer employs this image of breath as he encourages God's people to join with all creation in lifting their praise to God. The last verse concludes with these words: "Let everything that has breath praise the LORD. Praise the LORD." In other words, as the God who has given us life, we owe God our most heartfelt praise, as does all creation.

Today, as you go about your everyday affairs, look around you at the beauty of God's creation. Marvel at the magnificence at all God has brought about. Look in the mirror and celebrate your own existence. After all, God saw enough in you that he gave Jesus to be the means to your salvation. Most importantly, use your breath and your life to point others in his direction. Then may all creation share together in celebrating what God has made possible as we use our breath to glorify God.

Not in Ignorance

Acts 3:17-20

Now, fellow Israelites, I know that you acted in ignorance, as did your leaders. But this is how God fulfilled what he had foretold through all the prophets, saying that his Messiah would suffer. Repent, then, and turn to God, so that your sins may be wiped out, that times of refreshing may come from the LORD, and that he may send the Messiah, who has been appointed for you—even Jesus.

Sometimes I wonder if the most debilitating sins we commit are the ones we do in ignorance. The word ignorance has a negative connotation because of how it suggests that we are not smart enough to know how to come in out of the rain. But the word itself comes from the root word "to ignore," or the state of disregarding something. So, ignorance in its purest form has to do with something or someone we choose not to embrace.

In Acts 3, as the disciples of Jesus begin to fulfill the commission he gave them to bear witness to him to the uttermost parts of the earth, they begin in Jerusalem. Simon Peter has just healed a crippled beggar and the onlookers are amazed. Peter then takes the opportunity to illuminate them as to the power that made the healing possible, the power of the Risen Jesus flowing in and through him. Peter offers this explanation: "Brothers and sisters, I know you acted in ignorance, just as did your leaders." Then Peter goes on to explain how Jesus' death and resurrection fulfilled God's redemptive promises and that if they would turn from their ignorance and embrace Christ, they would experience forgiveness of all their sins and find refreshment for their souls.

It is very much the case that what people need the most is right before them, which is God's grace in Jesus Christ. The good news of the gospel is that God has made everything possible in Jesus to move beyond our pasts, so that we might seize the opportunity to experience the new and abundant life that God sent Jesus to bring.

I've often heard people say, "I could do God's will if only I knew it," which is in some way a confession of ignorance. Here's the place to begin: Confess Jesus. Be open to the power he makes possible. Be filled with his Spirit. Then you will know forgiveness of your sins and seasons of refreshing that will be sure to sustain you whatever comes your way.

Hear God's Voice

Psalm 95:6-7

Come, let us bow down in worship, let us kneel before the LORD our Maker;
for he is our God and we are the people of his pasture, the flock under his care.
Today, if only you would hear his voice.

Some years ago, a ministry colleague in another denomination gave me a copy of *The Book of Common Prayer*. We had been talking about spiritual formation, and I had indicated my desire to find a new resource that might help me reframe my devotional life. My friend offered me that resource, which I have used consistently for the last 10 or 15 years.

One of the prayers in the daily guide comes from Psalm 95, a prayer to be offered every day. (When you pray something every day, the words begin to sink in.) In this prayer we hear the psalmist call to the congregation: "Come and sing for joy to the LORD, shouting to him as the rock of our salvation." This psalm contains a phrase that has never failed to convict me: "Today, if you hear his voice." And then it goes on to warn us against repeating the mistakes of Israel in the wilderness as they rejected God's provision for their time of need.

But that phrase contains the conditional word "if." It's not a given that we will listen to God. Attending to God does not come automatically for us; it's not our default. We have to commit ourselves to doing so and to making it a priority. Sometimes we have to carve time out of our busy schedules to make time for God, and when we do, we wonder how we ever survived without doing so. The truth is, we couldn't survive without spending time with God. That's what I was confessing to my friend and colleague.

So, today, think about how well you're listening to God. After all, God is the rock of our salvation and the one who in Jesus gives us fullness of life. Listen to God today, for then not only will you survive whatever comes your way, but you also will thrive in the face of whatever comes your way. God will use it to serve his redemptive purpose for you, and in everything your soul will be formed more into the image of Christ until the day comes when for you all will be well.

Stay Humble as You Follow Jesus

Mark 14:27-31

"You will all fall away," Jesus told them, "For it is written: 'I will strike the shepherd, and the sheep will be scattered.' But after I have risen, I will go ahead of you into Galilee." Peter declared, "Even if all fall away, I will not." "Truly I tell you," Jesus answered, "today—yes, tonight—before the rooster crows twice you yourself will disown me three times." But Peter insisted emphatically, "Even if I have to die with you, I will never disown you." And all the others said the same.

There is a thin line between confidence and conceit. Confidence is a good thing; conceit is not. Confidence can sustain us when we find ourselves in challenging places; conceit will cause us to do foolish and desperate things. God can use our confidence, and Jesus can be honored in it. But our conceit only takes away from our witness and if unchecked, will destroy it.

That's one of the lessons in Mark's account of Jesus' confronting Simon Peter regarding what he thought was confidence but Jesus branded conceit. It was the last night Jesus was together with his disciples and also the occasion when he would tell them of his impending death. Peter, never the shy disciple, brashly interrupted Jesus by assuring him that Jesus would always be able to count on him. Peter would even be willing to die for him. As Mark 14 records, Jesus graciously but directly set Peter straight by predicting how before dawn of the next day, or as Jesus phrased it, before the rooster crowed, Peter would betray him three times. It would have been enough for me for Jesus to say, "You're going to deny me one time." But Jesus knew Peter had crossed the line from confidence to conceit, and so Jesus predicted rightly that Peter would betray him three times. Of course, Peter didn't accept it then; neither did the rest of the disciples. As verse 31 tells us, "And all the others said the same."

What would you have said? Actually, it doesn't matter what you'd say now, not in the private place where you're hearing this devotion. Your real answer will be given in the places you work and play, in the course of your everyday experience. So, it's best not to be too sure of yourself. It's better to understand that given the right circumstances, when the heat is turned up and the pressure is on, we all could deny Jesus. For if we check our egos and humble ourselves before Jesus, if we confess our need for his confidence and his courage, if we follow the example Jesus set for us in going to the cross—only then will we find the strength to stay with Jesus, regardless of what comes our way.

Today, as you allow Jesus to live through you, you'll be surprised at the confidence, not the conceit, that comes over you. It won't be yours, but rather what Jesus brings about in you. Then you can say that whatever challenges you come across today, "I can do all things through Christ who gives me strength."

Give Others Something Good to Talk About

Acts 8:4-8

Those who had been scattered preached the word wherever they went. Philip went down to a city in Samaria and proclaimed the Messiah there. When the crowds heard Philip and saw the signs he performed, they all paid close attention to what he said. For with shrieks, impure spirits came out of many, and many who were paralyzed or lame were healed. So there was great joy in that city.

It is a fact of human nature that we are going to talk about one another. Sometimes we talk well of others, but sometimes not so well. When our talk is harsh or critical, we call that "gossip." And no one likes to think of him or herself as a gossip.

But did you know that the word gossip and the word gospel come from the same root in Middle English meaning "to spread?" Which begs the question, "What are we spreading?" We do, after all, have a choice.

I think about the similarities between gospel and gossip when I read some of the stories in Acts, for example, the one about Philip in chapter 8. Philip had felt led to go to Samaria to proclaim the message of Jesus. Remember, the Jews avoided Samaritans like the plague because of how the Samaritans had compromised their purity by intermarrying with their foreign neighbors after the Northern Kingdom had fallen to the Assyrians. Yet Jesus did not avoid Samaria in his ministry; in fact, he commissioned his disciples to go to Jerusalem, Judea, *Samaria*, and the uttermost parts of the earth. Philip, then, was only doing what Jesus had told him to do. As Philip spoke his faith and lived his faith, the people "paid close attention to what he said," and great joy came to their city. And the gospel spread, or dare I say, the gospel "gossiped."

When people see your faith, what do they say about it? Does it bring joy to the place God has sent you? Today, be an instrument of God's peace and give people something good to talk about. Then the good news of Jesus will spread even more into the world and the joy of God's salvation will abound for others, even as clearly it abounds for you.

Follow Jesus for All the Right Reasons

Acts 8:18-24

When Simon saw that the Spirit was given at the laying on of the apostles' hands, he offered them money and said, "Give me also this ability so that everyone on whom I lay my hands may receive the Holy Spirit." Peter answered: "May your money perish with you, because you thought you could buy the gift of God with money! You have no part or share in this ministry, because your heart is not right before God. Repent of this wickedness and pray to the LORD in the hope that he may forgive you for having such a thought in your heart. For I see that you are full of bitterness and captive to sin." Then Simon answered, "Pray to the LORD for me so that nothing you have said may happen to me."

Righteousness involves doing the right things for the right reasons. Sometimes we can do things that are right, but we might be doing them for wrong reasons. And God hasn't said he would honor that. God will only find favor with our words and deeds when they stem from a pure heart, not a selfish and impure one.

The classic example of what I'm talking about is the story that's recorded in Acts 8, where a sorcerer-magician, named Simon comes to faith in Jesus. When the apostles hear about the remarkable occurrence, they dispatch Peter and John to Samaria to see what God has made possible.

The text tells us that the Samaritans had professed faith in Jesus, but they had not yet received the Holy Spirit. So, when Peter and John began laying hands on these converts and the Spirit came upon them, Simon the sorcerer was so impressed that he wanted to purchase their power. "How much does that cost?" is what he essentially asked them. Peter was not impressed. He told Simon where he could go and take his money with him (literally, that was Peter's response). Because God's power is a gift and God gives it only to those whose hearts are pure enough to employ it.

Could this be the main reason why so many people lack divine power today? Their hearts are not pure enough to employ it? Could that be a challenge you face because you think that someone serving God might also serve your interests? If so, confess that sin immediately. Ask God to purify your heart. Pray for the Holy Spirit to fill you and indwell you. For when the Spirit does so, there will be so much of Jesus in you that there won't be any room for self to stand in the way. The result will be something money could never buy: the joy of making a difference for Jesus and the knowledge that your life's priority is to hunger and thirst after God's righteousness, or always to do right things for the right reasons, a motivation that will make Jesus most proud.

Awaken Your Might

Psalm 80:1-2

Hear us, Shepherd of Israel, you who lead Joseph like a flock.
You who sit enthroned between the cherubim,
shine forth before Ephraim, Benjamin and Manasseh.
Awaken your might; come and save us.

Over the years I've heard many people speak of God as being an "on time" God, which is to say that God always seems to show up just at the moment we need him the most. Certainly, when you read Scripture, you see instance after instance where God does just that. God shows up to save the day and ultimately God shows up to save a life.

Sometimes, however, we find ourselves in situations where it seems that God has forgotten about us. Maybe it's because our lives seem to be so inconsequential in the face of all God has to deal with, we think that God is busy with other needs and has left us to stew in our own struggles. When those times come, we feel more than a little guilty for discounting God's compassion for us, but that's honestly how we feel. Maybe some of you are such a place today.

If so, then you'll appreciate the prayer voiced in Psalm 80, where the Psalmist prays for God to "awaken his might" and draw near to deliver him. The Psalmist calls upon the "Shepherd of Israel who leads Joseph like a flock." He refers to God as the one who sits enthroned "between the cherubim." He pleads with God to "awaken his might" and come to his defense that he and all the people may be saved from their distress.

What I find inspiring about Psalm 80 is the manner in which, as the Psalmist prays for God to rouse up and respond to his circumstance, he realizes that it's not so much that God has been asleep at the switch as it is that he has not been as mindful of God's presence and participation in his circumstances as he should have been. By pleading with God to "awaken his might," the Psalmist is actually arresting his own soul to the possibilities of what God can bring about if he simply would be open to them.

So, perhaps today you feel as if God has left you to your circumstances while he is off governing and directing other people's problems. Remember, God is not bound by the same constraints as we are. God is not limited by space and time. God is not overburdened and overwhelmed by everyday realities. Most importantly, God is not asleep at the switch. He who watches over Israel neither slumbers nor sleeps. So, be awake to what God can do for you and be open to the possibilities of the changes God can bring about in your life. God's provisions are always "on time," and his salvation is sufficient to save this day and every day.

Sow in Peace and Reap a Harvest of Righteousness

James 3:18

Peacemakers who sow in peace reap a harvest of righteousness.

Many people today are bemoaning the fact that our society is so polarized and divided. I know that we have never experienced anything near total unity as a country, but it does seem that people are more at odds with one another than at any other time I can remember.

To me, the worst part about it is how Christians don't seem to be contributing positively to any sort of resolution. If anything, we bear much responsibility for how things have gone sideways. For example, consider how our standing as evangelicals in general and Baptists in particular has declined, in large measure because of how we have been the fiercest of soldiers in today's culture wars. Now, I'm all for standing on principles and—to use the language of Jude—"earnestly contending for the faith once delivered to the saints." But don't you think we can do so without driving others away? I do.

Evidently, so did the author of the book of James. In chapter 3, James, the brother of Jesus and a leader of the Jerusalem church, urges his readers to be peacemakers who sow in peace so that they might reap a harvest of righteousness. The believers to whom James wrote were in the minority in their first-century world. They were not in the "driver's seat," so to speak. Yet from that minority position, James urged them to reach out to their neighbors, both Christians and unbelievers, offering them a witness that might honor the cause of Christ by spreading harmony, not discord.

We may rue the fact that our world today seems to be increasingly more hostile to faith, so much so that our status is moving in the direction from being in the majority to the minority. Perhaps that's God's way of humbling us so that we may point people beyond ourselves to Jesus and lean upon his power to make every place a more peaceful one.

Today, as you go about your business, think about sowing some seeds of peace. Scatter those seeds far and wide so that others may see you as one of God's children and your soul will be blessed because of how you are advancing Christ's cause in our troubled and divided world. You will be lifting up Jesus and not bringing him down. Because that is simply what righteous people truly do.

Show Your Love by Keeping Christ's Commands
John 14:21

Whoever has my commands and keeps them is the one who loves me.
The one who loves me will be loved by my Father,
and I too will love them and show myself to them.

One of the drawbacks to a grace-based religion is that we sometimes act as if works have no place. This position is what Dietrich Bonhoeffer, the famed World War II German theologian, referred to as "cheap grace"—all gift, no task. Bonhoeffer wasn't intending to discount the wonder of grace. He was instead elevating it by encouraging Jesus followers to live more into grace by allowing its power to drive their behavior. In other words, the surest sign of our salvation in grace is the manner in which we allow that grace to move us to live for Jesus.

Jesus spoke about this truth as it's recorded in John 14. You'll remember that chapter as containing the promise, "let not your hearts be troubled." As part of his last teaching to his disciples prior to his death on the cross, Jesus laid out for them his expectations for how they were to live in his love and show their gratitude for his grace. "Whoever has my commands," he said, "and keeps them is the one who loves me." Jesus wanted to see in his disciples not just words about how much they loved him; he wanted to see actions that gave evidence of it.

So, what does Jesus see in you? It's easy to sing "Oh, how I love Jesus." It's much harder to show it. But then, that's precisely where grace comes in. Grace empowers us to live in love as we keep Jesus' commands.

Today, live for Jesus not in order that Jesus might love you. Live for Jesus because he loves you and lives within you. Then, just as people in the first century said of those early Christians, so people in the 21st century will say of you, "We know they are Christians by their love."

See Others as God Sees Them

Acts 10:34

Then Peter began to speak:
"I now realize how true it is that God does not show favoritism."

Not many years ago, in his bestselling book, *Blink*, author Malcolm Gladwell reminded us of how quickly we form impressions of others. Gladwell wrote about how he had been on the receiving end of such judgments, which caused him to think about how often he did the same thing with other people. It's human nature evidently to come up with associations about other people that may or may not be true. If you've ever formed an opinion about someone that you came to see was false, you know how horrible the truth makes you feel.

So, wouldn't it be better if we could just be open to people as they are, even if our opinion of them wasn't sterling at the start? Of course, it would. But that human nature thing won't allow us to do so. For us to get to that point in our associations, something supernatural has to happen within us, something of God that enables us to see others as God sees them.

In Acts 10, as the good news of Jesus is making its way to the ends of the earth, a signal moment of expansion happens as the Holy Spirit instructs Simon Peter to go to the home of a Gentile centurion named Cornelius. At first Peter doesn't want to go. He's formed an impression of people similar to Cornelius. But in a dream God instructs Peter not to call unclean what God has deemed clean. Peter then decides to go to Cornelius' house and share with him the good news. To Peter's amazement, Cornelius responds positively and in the process Peter comes to see an important lesson. God is no respecter of persons. God doesn't play favorites. God is open to everyone. God sees all persons as precious in his sight. And the implication is, so should we.

I don't know how you see others. I know how I do. I have to admit that, as Gladwell said, I tend to form first impressions that aren't always based in reality. I need God to help me see others as he sees them so that I can better introduce them to the Jesus who died for their sins in the same way he died for mine. I invite you to do the same. Then we will see that all persons are God's favorites, red and yellow, black and white, and together in Christ we can be what God wants us to be—one great fellowship throughout the whole wide earth.

ORDINARY TIME

Use Your Gifts to Do God's Work
1 Corinthians 12:4-7

There are different kinds of gifts, but the same Spirit distributes them.
There are different kinds of service, but the same LORD.
There are different kinds of working, but in all of them and in everyone
it is the same God at work.

The matter of spiritual gifts is one of the most neglected of topics in Christian discipleship. For some reason, too many people think their gifts are underdeveloped or don't matter. It's not so much that some believers don't think they possess any. After all, we in the church have done a pretty good job of helping people see that everyone who belongs to Jesus has at least one spiritual gift. It's more the case that some don't think their gift matters much. Nothing could be further from the truth.

The topic of spiritual gifts is most emphatically addressed in Paul's first letter to the Corinthians. A dysfunctional church, the church at Corinth was sideways in almost every respect. So the Corinthians wouldn't be at odds with one another, Paul suggested that each person concentrate on using their gifts to promote Jesus. In chapter 12 he underscores how there are many gifts, but they all come from the same Spirit. There are different kinds of service, but they come from the same LORD. There are different kinds of work, but God is in it all. It doesn't take much to recognize a Trinitarian flow to Paul's teaching. The Spirit, Son, and Father are all invested in us through these gifts of grace so that God's purposes may be played out in this world.

The point is that all of God is at work in each of us. No matter our gift, God has granted it to us so that we might have something to contribute to Kingdom purposes. No gift is insignificant; every one counts. And because each gift stems from God, it doesn't matter how good you may think you are at employing it. Because God is in it, God will see that much comes from it.

So, today, think about how you might allow God to work through you. See your gift as one filled with the Spirit, redeemed by the Son, and brought to pass by the Father. Know that all of God is in you so that all of you may be in God. Then your life will be healthy and holy, and you can know that you are making a difference in the work of God that matters the most.

A Name for God

Genesis 11:3-4

They said to each other, "Come, let's make bricks and bake them thoroughly." They used brick instead of stone, and tar for mortar. Then they said, "Come, let us build ourselves a city, with a tower that reaches to the heavens, so that we may make a name for ourselves; otherwise, we will be scattered over the face of the whole earth."

The story of the Tower of Babel has always fascinated me. According to the book of Genesis, at one point the earth had one language and a common speech. Then one day, people came together and concocted a plan to work together to build a tower that stretched into the heavens. It wasn't so much the tower that got them in trouble with God—God is not opposed to being in fellowship with his people—but it was their desire "to make a name for ourselves and not be scattered over the face of the earth." They wanted to secure their sense of community by doing something that would put them on par with God. Therein lay their mistake. We as humans are not on par with God. To think that we can be is arrogance in the highest form.

So, God confused their language and the people were no longer able to work with one another. They became scattered, a division whose reality we live with to this day. But that's not the end of the story, at least not as far as God is concerned.

On the day of Pentecost, according to the book of Acts, the Holy Spirit fell on the believers in Jesus and they spoke the good news of Jesus in a way that everyone who had gathered in Jerusalem could understand—in spite of where they had come from and the language they spoke. It was the power and the presence of the Holy Spirit upon the believers that brought about a reversal of the Babel story.

In the letters of Paul that same Holy Spirit would join Jesus-followers together in a way that would enable them to build something eternal, not for themselves, but for their LORD and Savior; a community of faith, the church, that would elevate the name of Jesus throughout the earth.

If you're a Christian, you are blessed with that same Holy Spirit. In fact, no one can name Christ as Savior and LORD and not be filled with the Holy Spirit. You may not speak the same literal language, but if Jesus lives in you, then you can and must speak the same heart language, a language of mercy and grace so that you can join with other Christians to make the kingdoms of this world become the kingdom of our LORD and Christ.

So, secure your place in this world not by trying to make a name for yourself but instead by being open to the possibilities of how you might name Jesus in your everyday conversations and help others understand the importance of what God sent Jesus into this world to do—to forgive our sins and make possible our salvation. Then you will be a part of something holy and be worthy of the name "Christian," even that name that is above all other names, the name before which one day every knee shall bow and every tongue confess the very same thing: that Jesus Christ is LORD, to the glory of God the Father.

Breathe Freely and Faithfully

Ezekiel 37:7-8

So I prophesied as I was commanded. And as I was prophesying, there was a noise, a rattling sound, and the bones came together, bone to bone. I looked, and tendons and flesh appeared on them and skin covered them, but there was no breath in them.

We've all had the experience of having the breath knocked out of us. That's not a pleasant experience and every time it happens, for a moment we get into a panic and wonder if we'll ever be able to "catch our breath." But eventually we do and then everything gets back to normal. But for those few moments when we can't, it gets scary.

We tend to take our breath for granted. Do you ever pay attention to your breathing? Chances are, unless something is seriously wrong, you don't. But maybe you should, beginning with what it means to have the capacity to breathe freely and where that capacity came from in the first place.

The Hebrew word used for breath and Spirit is the same: it represents the gift of life. In Ezekiel 37, it's the animating power of the presence of God that transforms lifeless corpses into a vast army.

We are very aware of how today the cause of Christ needs strong and faithful soldiers to bear witness to God's kingdom purposes. The prevailing culture doesn't make living our faith easy, so sometimes things come along that take our breath away or that knock the props out from under. But when those challenges appear, we have the promise of God that through the Holy Spirit we are empowered for the challenges and able to win the day. As Paul reminded the church in Rome, we are more than conquerors through him who loved us and there is nothing that will ever separate us from that love.

So, if today you're going through a tough stretch, don't get anxious. Breathe freely. Breathe faithfully. Do that by living in the power of God's Holy Spirit, which will never leave you or forsake you. Come alive to the possibilities that only living for Jesus can bring your way.

Set Your Mind Right

Romans 8:5-8

Those who live according to the flesh have their minds set on what the flesh desires; but those who live in accordance with the Spirit have their minds set on what the Spirit desires. The mind governed by the flesh is death, but the mind governed by the Spirit is life and peace. The mind governed by the flesh is hostile to God; it does not submit to God's law, nor can it do so. Those who are in the realm of the flesh cannot please God.

Over the past couple of years, I've become ever more convinced that our ideological bent or mindset or frame of mind determines much of how we live each day. In other words, the way we perceive life to be ordered will inevitably show up in what we say and do.

This is why it's so important to approach everyday life from the standpoint of faith. If we believe that God has ordered life in such a way that all persons are to have equal opportunity to experience fullness and abundance, then as people of faith we are careful to do our part to encourage justice and equity and respect for all. But if we don't, then it's every person for herself, beginning with me. Just look at the conflicts that exist around us today and see where that ideological bent, that frame of mind, lands a soul. It's not good for anyone, even the person who thinks he's doing something for his own good.

So, how do we make sure that our actions coincide with our confession of faith? According to the Apostle Paul in Romans 8, we follow the lead of God's Holy Spirit: "Those who live according to the sinful nature have their minds set on what that nature desires, but those who live in accordance with the Spirit have their minds set on what the Spirit desires" (v. 5). It's a question of whether you follow God's heart or your own heart. And the best way to ensure that you're always on God's side is to open your life to the leadership of the Holy Spirit, whom Jesus himself said would lead us into all truth.

Today, you'll face some decisions that will have an impact on your life and the lives of others—some near and dear, some you may not know. But since none of us lives on an island, all of our actions have ripple effects that move far beyond our own souls. Make sure that in each decision you're being led by the Spirit, for only then will you be true to your faith and in concert with God's heart. Always make that your frame of mind, the manner in which you approach everything and everyone in life, and you will never miss out on any measure of God's favor in Jesus Christ—and neither will those with whom you cross paths.

In the Realm of the Spirit

Romans 8:9

You, however, are not in the realm of the flesh but are in the realm of the Spirit,
if indeed the Spirit of God lives in you.
And if anyone does not have the Spirit of Christ, they do not belong to Christ.

In our everyday conversations, we don't use the word "realm" very much. That's because it sounds "otherworldly." We talk instead about a field of study or an area of interest or a line of work. Maybe that's why I'm struck by the Apostle Paul's use of "realm" in Romans 8.

Paul, of course, wrote his letter to the Romans in Greek. But in the Greek the word realm is not mentioned. It's just Paul talking about being in the flesh or in the Spirit. To make sense of Paul's writing here, some translators have used the word realm to signify the mental and emotional space in which we live. They use it to refer to how we order our lives.

I like using the word realm to speak about what's required of us as Christians. The otherworldly nature of being filled and directed by the Holy Spirit resonates with me as being opposed to being driven by secular values. I also like the implications Paul draws from that thought: if you do not have the Spirit of God in you, then you do not belong to Christ. The defining characteristic of a Christian, therefore, is to be driven and directed by God's presence, empowering us to live in this world without buying into the world's values.

I trust you see what a realm of possibilities such an indwelling from above brings about. You're set free from living up to other people's expectations. You don't have to buy in to all the things that keep so many others awake at night. You are able to relate to everyone, even the people who don't look or think or even believe like you. You show the presence of Christ everywhere you go.

Today, dare to live in that realm, the realm of the Spirit—not the realm of the flesh. If you belong to Christ, you will, but not because it comes naturally to you, but because it comes supernaturally. It comes from God and is all the proof you should ever need that you truly belong to Christ.

Ardent, Not Lagging

Romans 12:11

Do not lag in zeal, be ardent in spirit, serve the LORD.

On Memorial Day we remember the ultimate sacrifice made by men and women in our armed forces who, as the hymn puts it, "loved liberty more than life." The freedoms we enjoy came about because of the willingness of so many to put their lives on the line for the good of their country. Truly, we should never forget their sacrifice.

We might call their service an "ardent" one: those brave soldiers held nothing back, but gave everything to the cause of freedom. Yes, if they had lagged in their zeal, they may have saved their own lives. But as Jesus taught his disciples, "What does it profit a man or a woman if they gain the whole world but lose their own souls." On Memorial Day we remember those who lost their lives, but did not lose their souls.

While none of us is likely to be required to show such sacrifice for our country, there is a sense in which we are expected to follow such an indelible example in living out our faith. The entirety of the Bible speaks to the high expectations God has for those who would serve his Kingdom purposes, and the New Testament offers up Jesus as the ultimate example of one who was obedient to death so that we might have life in all its abundance.

In Romans 8, Paul describes the power of the Holy Spirit to inspire us to such heights of service and offers this exhortation to the church: "Do not lag in zeal, but be ardent in spirit, serve the LORD" (v. 11). Then he gives us some instruction on how to do just that: "Rejoice in hope. Be patient in suffering. Persevere in prayer" (v. 12). In other words, the bookends of rejoicing in hope and perseverance in prayer keep our spirits up so that we might patiently endure whatever sufferings come our way. For we know, as Paul will say later in Romans 8, that "God works in all things for good for those whom he loves and who are called according to His purpose."

As we remember the ultimate sacrifice of those who served our country with valor and distinction, let us also remember Jesus who defined it for all the world. And let us follow his lead in the power of the Holy Spirit that we might gain so much more than we ever dreamed possible and be sure not to lose our own souls in the process.

Know Nothing But Jesus

1 Corinthians 2:2

For I resolved to know nothing while I was with you
except Jesus Christ and him crucified.

Some people would have you to think that "ignorance is bliss." The logic behind this saying is what you don't know won't hurt you. That may be true in part, but it's not the whole truth; and because it's not the whole truth, it will not set you free. There are some things we need to know so that we might be able to learn more important things.

For example, think about the earliest lessons you learned in elementary school: 1+1=2, the ABC's.... But you also learned important lessons such as how to get along with others and how to respect your elders. Robert Fulghum wrote a book built around the idea, *Everything I Needed to Know I Learned in Kindergarten*. I wouldn't go that far in my own life, but I would acknowledge that there are some foundational lessons that serve us very well as we grow and mature and become capable of learning more profound lessons.

That's also true in faith: Some lessons pave the way for us to grow as believers. The Apostle Paul states: "I resolved to know nothing while I was with you except Jesus Christ and him crucified" (1 Cor. 2:2). Paul wasn't bragging about what he didn't think he needed to know, in spite of the fact that some people in Corinth had branded him a fool. Rather, Paul wanted the Corinthians (and us) to see that until you understand life in the context of the cross, your so-called knowledge won't help you in the challenging moments of life. But if you begin with the understanding of God's power at work in the weakness of Christ crucified, then you see that God's power can work in your weakness and you learn to lean upon God instead of trusting in your own power.

Maybe today you've found yourself in a challenging place and can't find the knowledge to pull yourself out of the place that has you paralyzed. Go back to Calvary and remember what God did there. Reflect upon the power God showed in using that instrument of folly to provide the means to our salvation. Understand that if you start seeing your situation in light of what that power can do in you and through you, then you will know the truth—the fundamental truth, the life-giving truth, and that truth will set you free.

Blessed and Kept

Numbers 6:22-27

The LORD said to Moses, "Tell Aaron and his sons, 'This is how you are to bless the Israelites. Say to them: The LORD bless you and keep you; the LORD make his face shine on you and be gracious to you; the LORD turn his face toward you give you peace.'" "So they will put my name on the Israelites, and I will bless them."

The word benediction comes from a Latin word that means "blessing." We know it primarily as a closing prayer in a church service, but in truth it is much more. It is a word of favor bestowed upon faithful people, as they go out from sanctuary to service to make a difference for the cause of Christ.

There are many different benedictions in the Bible. Throughout the year I try to draw from them as we conclude worship and prepare to make that important transition from worship to service. For me it's a critical time in our gatherings. It's a time to recognize that much is at stake, that we're going out into an increasingly hostile world, and that we're not prepared in our own power for all that lies ahead. We need blessing to be sure.

My favorite one is known as the Blessing of Aaron, recorded in Numbers 6. Aaron was the brother of Moses and the high priest of the children of Israel. Although Moses was the leader of the faith community, Aaron had a special responsibility to mediate God's presence to the nation. In the book of Numbers, which all too sadly recounts the grumblings of Israel as the people wander through the wilderness, Moses instructs Aaron to bless the people in this way: "Tell them, 'May the LORD bless you and keep you. May the LORD make his face to shine upon you and be gracious unto you. May the LORD lift up his countenance upon you and grant you peace.'" I'm not sure the people received that blessing in the right spirit; for if they had, they wouldn't have grumbled as much as they did.

I'm not picking on the children of Israel. I grumble at times myself. That's why I need to be reminded of God's favor and the importance of being blessed and kept by God. I need God's presence in my life, God' grace and God's peace. My guess is that you do as well.

So be open to receiving this blessing. "May the LORD bless you and keep you. May the LORD make his face to shine upon you and be gracious to you. May the LORD lift up his countenance upon you and grant you his peace."

Have a Minute?

Behold the Glory

1 Samuel 4:21-22

She named the boy Ichabod, saying, "The Glory has departed from Israel"—because of the capture of the ark of God and the deaths of her father-in-law and her husband. She said, "The Glory has departed from Israel, for the ark of God has been captured."

In 1 Samuel 4, there is a deeply morose story that happens around the capture of the ark of the covenant by the Philistines and the distressing ripple effect it has on so many. The ark of the covenant was the gold-covered wooden chest the children of Israel crafted during their wilderness wanderings to be a sacred container for the tablets upon which God had inscribed his holy commandments. The ark became synonymous with God's presence with the nation as they fought battles and made their way into Canaan.

As Israel began settling the Promised Land, the ark was kept in Shiloh, the place of sanctuary. But when the Israelite fighters would go out to battle, they would carry the ark with them. On one such excursion at a place called Eben-ezer, the Philistines defeated Israel, captured the ark, and the nation was plunged into major distress.

As a consequence of that battle, Eli the priest's two sons, Hophni and Phineas died. Although neither son was a sterling soul, when word reached Eli and his family in Shiloh, Eli fell out of his chair, broke his neck and died. Phineas' wife also died, though not before giving birth to a son, whom she named Ichabod, which means "the glory of the LORD has departed from Israel."

God's glory did not depart because God wasn't capable of defending himself. In fact, in the subsequent chapter, God does just that. Plagues break out among the Philistines, and they end up returning the ark to Israel with gifts to go along with it. The glory departed because the people were not worthy of experiencing it, and its departure was a reminder that God's people should value his presence and not just see him as a good luck charm.

This story causes me to ask: "How do I see God? How do I value God?" Do I see God as a source I go to only as a last resort? Or do I see God as one in whom I should live and move and have my being?

None of us is worthy of experiencing God's glory, which is why God sent Jesus into the world. As John 1 puts it, "We beheld his glory, speaking of Jesus, glory of the Only Begotten, glory full of grace and truth." God sent Jesus to show us grace for our unworthiness and truth to guide us into the good future he has for us.

Today, you'll have battles you'll probably have to fight. That's life. But with your life centered in God, you'll experience victory. That's faith. You'll have victory not because you deserve it, but because Jesus has secured it. Faith is the victory that overcomes the world, and the glory of the LORD will always be with us as we trust in Christ so that nothing will ever separate us from his love in Christ Jesus.

A Life Preserved

Psalm 138:7

Though I walk in the midst of trouble,
you preserve my life.

One of the great misconceptions of our faith is that once we embrace it, all our troubles suddenly disappear. I don't know how that misconception ever got started, because there's nothing in Scripture that promises us such an easy path through life. We're not promised a carefree existence, but we are promised a presence that goes with us in life and especially when we find ourselves in times of trouble. That is most definitely a truth we see from Genesis to Revelation.

In Psalm 138, David offers his praises to God, as he puts it in the first verse, "with all of my heart." That's David's way of saying that he praises God with the entirety of his being. There's not one part of David's life that does not exalt the name of God, because there is not one part of David's life that is removed from God's presence and God's protection. In verse 7, David makes a bold but faithful claim: "Though I walk in the midst of trouble, you persevere my life." David had enemies before him and behind him, to his left and to his right, and at times even within his own family. But God was also there with David, every step of his way.

God will be present with you today and will preserve you. God's grace will abound precisely in those places where you are unable to overcome the challenge that has come your way. After all, we do not serve a weak, limited God. We serve a mighty God, the sovereign LORD of creation, the God who gave us life and has promised to preserve our life, the God and Father of our LORD Jesus Christ who proved by way of his only begotten son that nothing will ever separate us from his love, not even death itself.

So, don't let the troubles you face get you down. Instead, lean upon God's presence and power and let God lift you up. Just as did Jesus, into God's hands you commit your spirit, your soul, your heart, and your mind.

Claim God's Victory

1 Samuel 7:12

Then Samuel took a stone and set it up between Mizpah and Shen.
He named it Ebenezer, saying,
"Thus far the LORD has helped us."

In 1 Samuel 4 we read about one of the most devastating defeats Israel experienced. At Eben-ezer the Philistines overcame a great number of Israelite soldiers and made off with the ark of the covenant, the representation of God's presence with his people. In chapter 7 we read where Samuel gathers the people at Mizpah to confess their sins and prepare to do battle with the Philistines once again. How will it go? No doubt, the question was on all their hearts.

What I love about the story is the way Samuel, the prophet and judge, draws water, offers a sacrifice and then places a stone before the people, a stone he names Eben-ezer. Samuel shows his faith in God's ability to help Israel overcome the Philistines by claiming God's promise through the use of a name that represents the very place where Israel had suffered what was arguably its greatest defeat.

The name Ebenezer means "Thus far the LORD has helped us." And that's exactly what God did. God empowered the armies of Israel, and they defeated the Philistines: "So the Philistines were subdued and they stopped invading Israel's territory" (7:13). As long as Samuel lived, the Philistines were no more a threat.

A line in the hymn "Come, Thou Fount of Every Blessing" refers to this story: "Here I raise mine Ebenezer, hither by thy help I've come." I trust you know that promise in your life because you've trusted your life to God.

Today, you may be paralyzed by past defeats and disappointments, ones that like Eben-ezer have crushed your spirit and dashed your hopes. But God is not paralyzed. If you claim God's victory over those setbacks, God can propel you forward into the place of favor he has for you to know. So, whenever those memories come flooding back at you, painful as they are, give them to God. Raise your Ebenezer. Confess your faith that the God who has helped you to this point will help you going forward so that those memories will never haunt you again.

A Steadfast Heart

Psalm 108:1

My heart, O God, is steadfast;
I will sing and make music with all my soul.

The word steadfast is an important one in Scripture, and in the Old Testament is most associated with God, particularly God's steadfast love for his people. The concept of God's steadfast love is grounded in that of covenant, the notion that God has drawn near to his people to make a promise to protect and provide for them. God first made this promise with Abraham in the book of Genesis, and renewed the promise through his son, our Savior, Jesus Christ. Simply put, God's steadfast love means that God will never give up on us. We can always count on God.

But can God always count on us? Covenant is a two-way street. God makes promises to us, and God expects and deserves our steadfastness in return. But of course, we're fickle souls and sometimes we're not as committed, not as steadfast as we know we should be.

The concept of steadfast love shows up most frequently in the Psalms, so you wouldn't be surprised to see the idea of our reciprocating with our steadfast love to God in that book of the Bible. Many of the Psalms are attributed to David, and rightfully so. A man after God's own heart, David understood the importance of being steadfast before God. Yet, at times his faith wavered and his steadfastness with it.

So, how did David find the strength to be so steady in his devotion to God? Psalm 108:1 gives us a clue: "My heart, O God, is steadfast. I will sing and make music with all my soul." David shows us how and invites us to aside time to worship and praise God for his steadfast love to us. Because life gets busy and complicated, it's easy for other things to crowd out God, as important as God may be to us. We become so focused on the urgent that we sometimes lose track of the important, even the most important. But when we put God first and make our time with him a priority, then our hearts get to the place they need to be so that God's steadfast love works in us to give us the grace we need to tackle everything else that comes our way.

I trust that these devotions are helping you to do just that. Spending just a moment to focus on God's steadfast love for you in Jesus Christ will help you to show your love for God in return. So, offer some expression of praise and adoration to the God and Father of our LORD Jesus Christ who, through the presence of the Holy Spirit, shows steadfast love to us. There will be no better way for you to show the same to him.

Flourishing in the House of God

Psalm 52:8-9

But I am like an olive tree flourishing in the house of God; I trust in God's unfailing love for ever and ever. For what you have done I will always praise you in the presence of your faithful people. And I will hope in your name, for your name is good.

"Flourishing" is a powerful word. Taken from the world of botany, it suggests something that is bountiful and abundant and flowering. We would love for this word to characterize our own everyday existence. I don't know of anyone who wouldn't love to flourish.

To flourish, we must know the purpose for which we were created. A flower flourishes only when it blossoms into something it was supposed to show. Equally is that true for us as people created in the image of God. We flourish only when we live into the purpose for which we were created, which according to the Bible is to love God and serve his redemptive purposes.

In the last verses of Psalm 52, the Psalmist sings: "I am like an olive tree, flourishing in the house of God. I trust in God's unfailing name forever and ever. I will always praise you in the presence of your faithful people. And I will hope in your name, for your name is good." The Psalmist is comparing himself to deceitful men who think only of themselves and who prey off others to feed their own ambitions. They will not flourish; they will fail. More than that, they will wither and die. Yes, because they are evil, but more because they refused to serve the purpose for which God created them.

Today, you'll have a chance to serve God by living into the purpose for which you were created, and each of us was created by God to do something for his name's sake. Let praise be on your lips and in your heart as you move forward into this day. Before you know it, you'll begin to flourish, even if you don't feel like doing anything. If enough of us do that as faithfully as the olive trees in Israel, then God's purposes will come to pass, his name will be praised, and we will show our faithfulness that we might live as fully as we pray to live, today, tomorrow, and by God's powerful grace in Jesus Christ, forevermore.

Bearing Good Fruit

Luke 6:43-45

No good tree bears bad fruit, nor does a bad tree bear good fruit. Each tree is recognized by its own fruit. People do not pick figs from thornbushes, or grapes from briers. A good man brings good things out of the good stored up in his heart, and an evil man brings evil things out of the evil stored up in his heart. For the mouth speaks what the heart is full of.

There was a food truck in our neighborhood one day that featured nothing but fruit—no barbecue, no Mexican, no Asian, just fruit. The lines were long, because people love good fruit, especially at this time of the year. But what if the truck had been serving bad fruit, spoiled fruit, rotten fruit? How long do you think those lines would have been? Not long at all, and neither would it have been long until the food truck would have gone out of business. Its entire business model is based on serving up fruit that is pleasing to the eye and to the taste.

As Christians, do we understand how our business model is not that much different? Do we get how people today are looking to us for something that is pleasing and inviting, not spoiled and smelly?

I've been taken back at some of the ugliness that has gotten attached to the church's witness in general and the Baptist witness in particular, and it's reminded me of the importance of Jesus' words in Luke's gospel as to the type of witness Jesus wants to see from his disciples. In chapter 6, Jesus tells them: "No good tree bears bad fruit, nor does a bad tree bear good fruit. Each tree is recognized by its own fruit." Jesus was talking about a witness that is good and pleasant and true to seed that gave it life in the first place. He was talking about a witness that reflects positively on him.

So, what is your fruit saying about your faith in Jesus? And how do your words and deeds reflect Jesus' presence in your life?

Let that thought stay with you as you go about your everyday activities. People you come across need something nourishing and nurturing, something that will do them good. In a day when we in the church get all flustered about our future, best we concentrate on the fruit we're serving up in Jesus' name. If we get it right and bear witness to what is best about Jesus, people will line up to taste the difference he makes. Otherwise, we won't be in business much longer either.

Relief to Those with Evil Spirits

1 Samuel 16:23

Whenever the spirit from God came on Saul, David would take up his lyre and play.
Then relief would come to Saul; he would feel better,
and the evil spirit would leave him.

In the game of "rock, paper, scissors" there's no way to guarantee a win. Paper covers rock. Scissors cut paper. Rock pounds scissors. It's all left to chance as to who wins the day.

But in the contest between good and evil, there is no doubt in the long run which will prevail. Good will always win out over evil. It may take more time than we expect, but evil will not hold out against good forever. Ultimately, good will prevail. So, we need to make sure we are always on the side of good.

We see this principle played out in the story of David, when he was in the service of King Saul. Saul had become possessed by an evil spirit, and the evil spirit was holding sway over his being. His servants informed Saul about a shepherd boy from the house of Jesse who was a marvelous lyre player, who had this remarkable ability to calm anxious spirits and even evil ones.

Saul sent for David, and sure enough, as 1 Samuel 16 tells us: "Whenever the Spirit of God would come upon Saul, David would take up his lyre and play. Then relief would come to Saul; he would feel better, and the evil spirit would leave him." I find it interesting that 1 Samuel would conflate the evil spirit with the Spirit of God, but it was the author's way of assuring us that our good God is in control of everything and everyone and when God is present, evil takes a back seat.

I wonder at times as we moan and groan about the evil that exists in our world how might we, like David, bring comfort and peace to those afflicted by it? How might we use our gifts and talents to drive evil away? What might we do to bring to bear God's presence and power upon people and places where evil abounds?

I invite you to think about those possibilities and then to make yourself available for God to use you in those ways. Then, when evil attempts to cover or cut or pound, it will lose out to the power of good. It will lose out to the power of God, and you will be the instrument through which God's good will forever prevail.

Being Known for Who You Are

Psalm 8:16

The LORD is known by his acts of justice;
the wicked are ensnared by the work of their hands.

One of the benefits of growing up in a small town is that everyone there knows who you are. They know who you belong to. They know everything about you. But of course, others would say that's also a disadvantage. They know who you are. They know who you belong to. They know everything about you. The task, then, is to make sure that you keep your hands clean and stay out of trouble. That way, you have nothing to hide.

People don't seem to pay attention to reputation as much as they once did. I don't know exactly why. It could be that we've become so isolated from others that we don't worry about what they think of us. The smallness of community doesn't make how others perceive us seem to be as big of a deal as it once was.

That's unfortunate. Reputation ultimately speaks to character, and character reflects on those we love most. That was the message I learned growing up, especially when as I would leave the house, my parents would always tell me: "Remember who you are. Remember who you are."

Maybe today, we need a bit more remembering as we go out into the world.

In Psalm 9:16, the Psalmist speaks about how God is known by "his acts of justice." Meanwhile, others are "ensnared by the works of their hands." That is to say, when people throw reputation to the wind—especially those who belong to God—their lives are constrained and they miss out on so much of the favor God has for them. It would be better that they remember who they are and give themselves to acts of justice. And in the process they would not only free others to know the fullness of life, but would also free themselves.

So, today as you go out, remember who you are. And, remember whose you are. As the Apostle Paul reminded the Corinthians, "you were bought with a price," the shed blood of Jesus. You're a child of the King, so act like it. It's not just your reputation at stake; it's also God's. To disregard that reality will only hold you back from all the good God has for you to know.

Have a Minute?

Put Your Hope in God's Word

Psalm 119:114

You are my refuge and my shield;
I have put my hope in your word.

"What's the good word?" That's an expression many people used to say whenever they came across someone. The question was a conversation starter in one respect, but it was also a plea for some bit of information that might lift one's spirits in the face of all that life throws at us. "What's the good word?" The implication isthat if I can hold on to a good word, whatever comes my way, then that word will sustain me and see me through.

For people of faith, there is no better word than God's word. God's word never fails to calm our spirits, settle our souls, and excite our emotions. God's word, because it is steadfast and true, is a firm foundation for building a life.

Psalm 119, the longest chapter in the Bible, is a song of praise about the virtues of God's word. In verse 114, the Psalmist proclaims, "You are my refuge and shield. I have put my hope in your word." The Psalmist had discovered the ability of God's promises to give light in the midst of life's darkness and promise in the midst of life's despair.

I trust you've made the same discovery in your life. I find it remarkable how too many Christians assume they can live meaningfully without constantly aligning their lives with God's word. It is a truly perfect treasure of faith and of practice. It not only tells us what to believe, but it also tells us how to live our belief.

So, today, put your hope in God's word. In particular, put your hope in God's word that became flesh—his son, our Savior, the LORD Jesus. Let God's promises, perfectly fulfilled in Jesus, guide your every word and deed. Then you will find refuge and strength whenever you are confronted with some challenge. You will know the peace that passes all understanding by trusting your way to the One who will never let you down.

Loving God's Law

Psalm 119:113

I hate double-minded people,
but I love your law.

As people of grace, we are skeptical of the law. I'm not talking about the law of the land, those rules and regulations that make for a civilized society—even though there may be some of them we don't understand or fully support. I'm talking about the religious law, the law of Moses, the law handed down by God to his servant on Mount Sinai to guide the people into the land of promise and once there to govern their life so that they might flourish in all things.

As the New Testament reminds us, Jesus came not to abolish the law but to fulfill it. Somehow, we Christians have missed that part of our LORD's teaching. Because we've focused so intently on the Apostle Paul's writings, which were necessary for law not to override grace, we've thrown out the value of religious law altogether, in spite of the fact that even Paul said it was a schoolmaster meant to show us the error of our ways so that we might be driven to grace.

The Bible invites us to take a more comprehensive view of law so that we see it as God's clear expectations for his people. When we find ourselves at crossroads moments in life, God's law shows us the way and God's grace in Jesus Christ empowers us to fulfill it. Law and grace are two sides of the same coin, a coin we did not earn, so that we might live in a way that is pleasing to God.

In Psalm 119:13, the Psalmist speaks of how he hates double-minded people but loves the law of the LORD. Think about that for a moment. What is it about double-minded people the Psalmist couldn't stand? It was the fact that such people can't be trusted. You can't rely on them. They're one way today and another way tomorrow, and sometimes they change course multiple times in the course of a single day! But God's law is sure and certain. We can always count on it to lead us along paths of righteousness for his name's sake. And when we find that living into it is more than we can do in our own power, grace kicks in to help us in our weakness so that our lives might point others to the steadfast love God has for all through our LORD Jesus Christ. Thanks be to God that there's no law against that!

Ask God

Psalm 119:125

I am your servant;
give me discernment that I may understand your statutes.

Discernment is one of those words we don't pay attention to nearly enough. That's because it refers to an ability to see the meaning of what's going on all around us in any given moment. It suggests seeing something not only with the eyes, but also seeing them with the heart.

Nowhere does this gift of discernment apply more than to the matter of God's will. How many times have I heard someone say that they could do God's will if only they could know God's will? I understand what they're saying. Our spirits are truly willing even when at times our flesh is weak. But if our spirit lacks the direction the flesh needs, then what hope do we have?

You'll notice that I have referred to discernment as a gift. I believe that to be the case when it comes to the will of God. I will grant that when it comes to a lot of life, discernment is an art; it is something we can develop. But when it comes to the things of God, we are totally dependent on God to show us the way. The good news is that God is willing to do so. God does not intend for his will to be a constant mystery. But God does will that those who wish to know it are willing to bow before him in glad adoration.

Psalm 119 is chock full of guidance and inspiration for how we are to live as people of faith. In verse 125, the Psalmist proclaims this word: "I am your servant; give me discernment that I may understand your statutes." Notice how the Psalmist begins. "I am your servant." If he had not begun that way, then his plea would have sounded more like a demand. "Give me your discernment." But because he began in humility, he was confident that God would show him the way.

Perhaps today you are a bit befuddled as to how you are to proceed with your life. You need discernment. It's not that you can't see what's taking place. You need to see the meaning of what's taking place and more importantly where God is in all of it. Begin by humbling yourself. Then be certain that God will show you the way. If it doesn't happen as soon as you would like, stay with it. God's timing is perfect, just as is God's will. God's timing is good, acceptable, and perfect. And when you humble yourself before God and promise to serve him, then just as did Jesus, God will exalt you and bless you and bring about his redemptive purposes through you.

The Sorrow That Leads to Repentance

2 Corinthians 7:10

Godly sorrow brings repentance that leads to salvation and leaves no regret, but worldly sorrow brings death.

Apologies are hard to come by for most of us. That's because in order for us to apologize, we first have to acknowledge that we were in the wrong about something or someone—which is hard for a lot of us to do. We like to think of ourselves as good people. Oh, we know that we are not perfect people. But we are not entirely bad either, or so we would like to think.

That being the case, if there is any bad in our life, which as sinners we know there is, we will at some point along life's way not do right about something or someone. When those moments happen, it's important as people of faith to own up to that wrong and then to commit by God's grace not to repeat it. The Bible word for that action is repentance, which is more than remorse; it's resolve not to keep doing the same wrong things.

In his second letter to the Corinthians, Paul expressed his pain over how he had been falsely maligned by that fellowship. They had accused him of wrong teaching and wrong motivation. They had said he was only interested in power and money. In 2 Corinthians 7, Paul says he regrets the pain it caused them, but he praises God for what he says is the "godly sorrow" it provoked that led them to repentance." "Godly sorrow brings repentance that leads to salvation," Paul writes verse 10, "but worldly sorrow leads to death." In other words, if the Holy Spirit convicts you as to how you are in the wrong, your sorrowful response will then lead you to make amends. But if it's just the sorrow of mere human emotion, you'll keep making the same mistake until ultimately your mistakes will bring you to ruin.

You don't want that in your life, do you? Then pray for God to show you where you have been in the wrong about something or someone. Then let your faithful response to that revelation lead you to make amends. Doing so will bring about healing for you and for everyone and everything involved, which is what salvation ultimately means. Everything will be then made whole or at least a little closer to it, and with God's help through your faith in Christ, all will be well.

Have a Minute?

How to Give Yourself Away

2 Corinthians 8:1-5

And now, brothers and sisters, we want you to know about the grace that God has given the Macedonian churches. In the midst of a very severe trial, their overflowing joy and their extreme poverty welled up in rich generosity. For I testify that they gave as much as they were able, and even beyond their ability. Entirely on their own, they urgently pleaded with us for the privilege of sharing in this service to the LORD's people. And they exceeded our expectations: They gave themselves first of all to the LORD, and then by the will of God also to us.

Generosity has become a buzzword of sorts in our day. Even in business circles where those in charge monitor the bottom line, the realization has set in that people are prone to support those entities that exude generosity. Of course, churches have supported generous impulses from the beginning. Look at the book of Acts and how members willingly shared of their possessions to meet needs within the fellowship. But such generosity doesn't happen easily. People have to commit themselves to rising above their own instincts to fend for themselves, and even churches have to rely on the Spirit's inspiration to do so.

The Bible is full of generous souls, but perhaps none more than the Macedonian believers who had taken up an offering for the Apostle Paul to take with him to the poor saints in Jerusalem. Paul invited the Corinthian church to join in on the generosity, but they were finding it hard to be a part of the giving party. So, Paul pointed to the Macedonians, who in 2 Corinthians 8, he writes, "gave as much as they were able, and beyond their ability." That's the mark of generosity, is it not? So, how did they do it? Verse 5 shows us the answer: "They gave themselves first of all to the LORD, and then by the will of God to us." They saw themselves as giving to Jesus, who had given of himself to them on the cross. And seeing such love lavished upon their souls, what else could they do? They gave even out of their extreme poverty.

You may feel as if you don't have much at your disposal to show generosity. But understand, a spirit of generosity isn't based on mere math; it's based on gratitude. It's based on the realization that in Christ, God has given so much for you. It's based on your desire to do what you can with whatever you have so that others might experience the riches of Christ's grace, even as have you.

So, today, give yourself first to God. Then let the Spirit lead however the Spirit leads. You'll find your heart loosening up. You'll see opportunities to address pressing need. You'll know the joy of generosity. Most importantly, you'll be doing all of it in Jesus' name, the one who ultimately is the source of every good and perfect gift.

Look to Others to Help You Look to God

1 Samuel 23:15-18

While David was at Horesh in the Desert of Ziph, he learned that Saul had come out to take his life. And Saul's son Jonathan went to David at Horesh and helped him find strength in God. "Don't be afraid," he said. "My father Saul will not lay a hand on you. You will be king over Israel, and I will be second to you. Even my father Saul knows this." The two of them made a covenant before the LORD. Then Jonathan went home, but David remained at Horesh.

There is strength in numbers. Any time we find ourselves facing a challenging situation, it's best to have at least one person in our corner standing with us. Otherwise, the challenge may be more for us to handle by ourselves. But with someone at our side, we find encouragement and strength.

That's what David discovered in the season of his life when Saul, king of Israel, was hot on his trail because of Saul's jealousy over David's popularity with the masses. For a while Saul managed his hostility toward David, but as time went on, Saul couldn't handle his animosity. It got the best of him, and he decided to do away with David. Of course, what Saul didn't understand was that God had already chosen David to be Saul's successor and there was nothing Saul could do to change that inevitability—not that Saul didn't try.

In 1 Samuel 23, the story is told of how Saul had driven David into the wilderness of Ziph, where day after day Saul sought David out to kill him. But in the midst of Saul's hot pursuit of David, Saul's own son Jonathan came out to meet David and to encourage him. Verse 16 tells us that Jonathan went to David at Horesh and helped him find strength in God."

Perhaps today you need someone to help you find that same source of strength. Even if you can't think of anyone immediately, there are people who would love nothing more than to be there for you in your time of need. So, pray for God to reveal them to you, and then bless them by calling on them for their support. And if you still can't think of anyone, think of Jesus, the one friend who sticks closer than a brother. What a friend we have with Jesus! Remember that you are not alone. There is help at your disposal. Seek it out and be strong in the LORD.

Call in Your Distress

Psalm 18:6

In my distress I called to the LORD;
I cried to my God for help.
From his temple he heard my voice;
my cry came before him, into his ears.

Why is it that we seem to exhaust all other options before we decide to call on God? I guess it's human nature for us to do our best to fend for ourselves, but from what the Bible tells us, human nature is a sinful thing. We all have sinned and come short of the glory of God.

That's not a dig at the importance of being responsible people. I don't think there's anything in Scripture that doesn't allow us to take initiative and give our best effort, as long as we do so with God's bidding. It's when we get ahead of God and go our own way that we tend to get into trouble. But in those times when we do even that, we can be certain that God stands ready to hear our pleas and come to us in our distress.

In Psalm 18 the Psalmist, traditionally David, lifts a hymn of praise to God for how God has come to his aid and at the right time. Verse 6 puts it this way: "In my distress I called to the LORD. I cried to my God for help. From his temple he heard my voice; my cry came before him, into his ears." As David had learned, God is not confined to his throne up in heaven. God draws near to those who turn to him in their times of distress to do for them what they could never do for themselves.

Perhaps today you're in such a place. God sees you and is waiting on you to call for his help. When you do, God will draw near. Jesus is proof of God's heart to do so. In our Savior and LORD, God came down from his throne in glory to redeem humans who were hopeless and hapless and make for them a way even when a way didn't seem possible.

God can do the same for you. Your cries will not fall on deaf ears; they will fall on divine ones. Now, get ready for God to do for you even this day immeasurably more than you might even ask or imagine.

Trust and Don't Be Shaken

Psalm 21:7

For the king trusts in the LORD;
through the unfailing love of the Most High he will not be shaken.

Trust me when I tell you that everyone has a yellow streak down their back, a yellow streak as big as a highway stripe. You know what that phrase means; do you not? It means that all of us have those things that keep us awake at night and in the morning and in the evening. All of us are afraid of something…or of someone. People may try to tell you otherwise, but they're only trying to trick you, and it may be that they're trying to trick themselves as well.

Owning up to our fears is the first step in overcoming them. At some point you have to confront what you're afraid of in order to rise above it. But it also helps when you confront it that you do so in the presence of another. What better presence to have at your side as you face your fears than the Almighty and Everlasting God?

In Psalm 21, the king extols God for his goodness and protection. God has placed him on the throne, but God hasn't left him there to fend for himself. As enemies have arisen to challenge his reign, God has provided the resources to overcome them at every turn. Verse 7 puts it this way: "For the king trusts in the LORD, through the unfailing love of the Most High he will not be shaken."

It wasn't that the king was crowing over his innate courage. No, the king had threats that made him very afraid. But instead of giving in to those threats, the king had decided to give them to God. The result was that even in the face of his many challenges, he could stay steady and strong. With God's unfailing love he would not be shaken.

I hope you can say that in your experience. I hope you can look at the things that give you pause and know that as they come your way you won't be on your own. God will be with you, the God and Father of our LORD Jesus Christ, who in his Son our Savior displayed a power that overcame every enemy, even the one who gives us the most pause—death itself! You have nothing to be afraid of if you trust in God's unfailing love. His love will never let you go. You will be kept safe even to the end, and every moment until that time comes will be one of victory.

So, today, trust in God's unfailing love, even and especially when fear starts to creep into your heart. Perfect love casts out all fear, and that love can be perfected in you as you follow its full manifestation in Christ Jesus.

Where Shall We Go?

2 Samuel 2:1

In the course of time, David inquired of the LORD. "Shall I go up to one of the towns of Judah?" he asked. The LORD said, "Go up." David asked, "Where shall I go?" "To Hebron," the LORD answered.

Whenever we find ourselves in a place where we don't know our way around, it's always best that we ask for directions. Of course, as a man, I know that it's my bound duty to try to orient myself to the new conditions. But having attempted that and failed on far too many occasions than I care to admit, I have come to a place in my life where I don't hesitate to ask.

That's especially important when we find ourselves at a place in life where only God knows the way forward. I'm talking about those moments when we know that if we took a wrong turn, we might miss out on the good that God has in store for us to experience. So, learning how to follow God's lead is the first requirement in coming to abundant life.

In 2 Samuel 2, David has come to one of those moments in his own life. Saul has been killed in battle, and there is a vacancy on the throne. Because God had told David long ago that he would rule over the house of Israel, David knew that he didn't need to take a wrong path. So, he asked God where he should proceed. God's response? Hebron. Not Gibeah, where Saul had established his throne. Not Bethlehem, David's hometown. Not Jerusalem, which wasn't yet a city of prominence for God's people. Hebron. So, there David went until the elders of Israel arrived to anoint him king.

Many times in life we get the idea that we know how we should proceed even we don't. The end result is that we get ahead of God, which was Saul's mistake when he showed impatience with the prophet Samuel's request. Don't you do that. Trust your way to God, even as did David, and especially as did the Son of David, our LORD Christ. God will show you the way. At the end of it will be blessing, more blessing than you thought possible; blessing made possible by God's amazing grace, grace that takes us from where we are lost and directs us to a place where we might be found.

Not by Appearances

2 Corinthians 10:7-11

You are judging by appearances. If anyone is confident that they belong to Christ, they should consider again that we belong to Christ just as much as they do. So even if I boast somewhat freely about the authority the LORD gave us for building you up rather than tearing you down, I will not be ashamed of it. I do not want to seem to be trying to frighten you with my letters. For some say, "His letters are weighty and forceful, but in person he is unimpressive and his speaking amounts to nothing." Such people should realize that what we are in our letters when we are absent, we will be in our actions when we are present.

You really cannot judge a book by its cover, and you can't judge people by the way they look. That's actually more the case with the latter than the former. Sometimes if there's enough information on the cover of the book, we can figure out what the contents are about. But we can never know a person's heart by looking at him purely on the outside. Sometimes we have to be reminded of that fact.

In 2 Corinthians, Paul reminded believers not to allow his unimpressive appearance to get in the way of the godly instruction the Spirit had inspired him to give. Evidently, Paul wasn't much to look at. But when you read Paul's writings you see that his heart was pure and powerful. So, in chapter 10, Paul admonishes the church for thinking that he was weak and ill-informed to offer anything of good to believers in such an impressive city like Corinth. "If anyone is confident they belong to Christ," he writes, "they should consider that we belong to Christ just as much as they do."

Today, you'll bump into people, some of whom by appearance will be impressive and some not. You won't be able to tell the whole story by how they look. Instead, begin with the assumption that they will have something to offer—and everyone does. Then you may in the course of your interactions see more from them than you ever bargained for, something that will add to your life and your faith and make you more of the person that God in Christ needs you to be.

Weak, and Proud of It

2 Corinthians 11:30

If I must boast,
I will boast of the things that show my weakness.

We all learned growing up that it's not polite to boast. No one likes a braggard. No one wants to hear how great you think you are because of how such boasting either makes others feel small or it makes you seem untruthful. Oh, I know the saying, "No brag; just fact." But it's always best to let your actions speak for themselves so that you don't put other people off with your words.

But in 2 Corinthians, the Apostle Paul speaks of another type of boasting, one wherein we boast of our weakness. In this letter, Paul writes to defend his calling to the church, a calling that some have seen as a most boastful one. In chapter 11, as Paul takes on the charge, he explains that instead of boasting from a worldly perspective in which one applauds one's own strength, Paul has felt compelled to boast of his weakness, for when he speaks of his frailties, he's acknowledging how any strength he possesses comes through his faith in Christ.

While I appreciate the decorum we've been taught never to boast about our strengths to others, I don't know that it's necessarily helpful to us to dismiss our talents, our abilities, and even our accomplishments. But as Christians, I do think Paul helps us to see that as we speak of those things, we best do so by pointing beyond ourselves to Jesus. If we are anything—and each of us is most definitely something—it's because we're people created in the image of God, folks whom Jesus is redeeming, and recipients of a grace that is sufficient for our every need.

So, today, boast of your weakness so that the strength of Christ at work in you might be more evident. Then, others won't be put off by your witness; they'll be attracted to it. Most importantly, they'll want to know more of this Jesus who is the source of your strength, assurance, and joy.

Patient in Suffering

James 5:10-11

Brothers and sisters, as an example of patience in the face of suffering, take the prophets who spoke in the name of the LORD. As you know, we count as blessed those who have persevered. You have heard of Job's perseverance and have seen what the LORD finally brought about. The LORD is full of compassion and mercy.

Patience and suffering are two words that most of us would prefer never to have to use, and certainly not in the same breath. Either one is bad enough on its own, but when you combine the two, we can't think of a worst fate.

Part of our struggle is our desire to be in control when those moments of suffering come our way, which they inevitably do for everyone. Then what little patience we might have had gets exhausted, and all hope of controlling our situations goes out the proverbial window.

But what if the secret to maintaining our patience in the face of suffering wasn't a matter of our trying to control our circumstances at all? What if the secret lay instead in our relinquishing control to a God whose plans for his people will inevitably come to pass, plans to bless us and keep us and favor us with a good future?

In the book of James there is much talk of how to live one's faith in Jesus and not just to talk about it. "Be ye doers of the word and not hearers only," as James reminds us in chapter 1. And to his credit, James understood how doing the word could often land believers in a hard place, though one that was still marked by the abiding presence of Jesus.

In chapter 5, James speaks to the church about the importance of showing patience in the midst of our sufferings by trusting our situations to God, as have all the heroes of the faith throughout time, including the prophets and Job, and for that matter Jesus. Each of those persons trusted their situations to God instead of trying to stay in control of them, and their stories all ended with God coming through with vindication and favor and resurrection.

God can do the same in our situations, James tells us, because as James 5:11 reminds us, "The LORD is full of compassion and mercy." The LORD has enough compassion and mercy to calm our souls and sustain us in our sufferings. So, if your lot in life becomes more than you bargained for and impossible for you to control, let go and let God. Only then will you find the strength to see you through that tough time to a better one, a time marked by vindication and favor and everlasting life. It will surely be worth the wait.

Wait for Your Time

John 7:6-9

Therefore Jesus told them, "My time is not yet here; for you any time will do. The world cannot hate you, but it hates me because I testify that its works are evil. You go to the festival. I am not going up to this festival, because my time has not yet fully come." After he had said this, he stayed in Galilee.

Time is a peculiar and flimsy notion. On one hand, we live by the clock, waiting for the time to come to tick things off our to-do lists. On the other hand, we don't have enough time to get everything we want to do accomplished. Sometimes there just doesn't seem to be enough hours in the day.

But there's also a sense in which we talk about "the right time," which is something that cannot be measured by any device. It's the precise moment when God's will becomes most apparent to us and we find ourselves inspired to be obedient to it.

You see this concept of the "right time" throughout the Bible, but nowhere more apparent than in John's gospel, where Jesus speaks of "his hour" or "his time." In those moments Jesus is speaking about the looming cross and his awareness of how that emblem of suffering and shame is God's will for him, and it is God's will for the world. Everything in Jesus' life is ordered around that cross so that throughout the Fourth Gospel, Jesus is reluctant to be pushed into doing anything that would cause him to move outside of God's plan or even worse to get ahead of it.

In John 7, Jesus' brothers tempt him to go to Jerusalem for the Feast of Tabernacles, one of the three signal feasts in Jewish life, but Jesus is concerned that to do so would be to step outside God's purpose. So, Jesus declines. "My time is not come. For you, any time will do. But not for me." And so, he stays in Galilee. Of course, later Jesus does go. But he doesn't want his brothers to perceive that somehow, they have talked him into doing so. Jesus wanted nothing but for his life to be marked by obedience to God.

Is that how you want your life to be marked, or do you find yourself being driven by the thoughts and suggestions of others? Sometimes we need a little push from others, but at all times we need to make sure that the greatest urgency in our life is that which is marked by God's will.

Today, you'll be involved with many important tasks and responsibilities, and the clock will most likely be driving you. But in the midst of it all, sense how your activity is reflecting your obedience to God and God's purpose in your life. There is a time and a place for everything, especially for the will of God. And when you live mindful of that truth, then when your time comes, you will be ready to do what God gives you to do; in that moment you will know life and know it most abundantly.

Encouraging Others to Know Christ
Colossians 2:1

My goal is that they may be encouraged in heart and united in love, so that they may have the full riches of complete understanding, in order that they may know the mystery of God, namely, Christ, in whom are hidden all the treasures of wisdom and knowledge.

Faith is something we are to pass on to others. All the riches of grace that have come to us through our devotion to Jesus are not to be hoarded and kept to ourselves. We are to share them freely so that we might have company as we come boldly before God's throne of grace.

How do we best do that without imposing our will on others? How do we help others recognize all they stand to gain by drawing near to Jesus without coercing them in any way? This task seems to be the real challenge of our present day when speaking about our faith can just as easily be termed "hate speech" as "grace speech."

One approach is to follow the Apostle Paul's lead as he explained his heart to the church at Colossae. Paul's letter to the Colossians was directed to a church he never actually visited, which makes that epistle different from the others Paul wrote. Every other letter was intended for a church Paul had a direct relationship with, but Colossae was a place where Paul had only learned of their devotion to Jesus at second-hand. Therefore, he sensed the need to inform his readers that his only goal, as he phrases it in the second chapter of his letter, "was to encourage them in heart and unite them in love so that they might have the full riches of complete understanding, in order that they may know the mystery of God; namely, Christ." Paul knew the Colossian community was steeped in mystery religion, the devotion to esoteric ideas. So instead of admonishing them to turn away from such interests, Paul met them where they were and showed them the deeper truths of Jesus.

We live in a day when people seem to be interested in everything but Jesus. Turning their attention in his direction won't be successful if we assume an arrogant or condescending tone to our message. We can only be successful if we mirror Paul's approach and show encouragement and love. So, why not do that today through your words and your deeds so that others may come to a more complete understanding of all that Jesus has to offer for their everyday experience. And, as you help others to come to that understanding, so will you also.

Grace Talk

Colossians 4:6

Let your conversation be always full of grace, seasoned with salt,
so that you may know how to answer everyone.

The Bible is clear that if we are not careful, our tongues can get us into big trouble. Words are similar to arrows: once released, they can never be recovered. So, we need to be thoughtful about what we say before we say it.

Paul's letter to the Colossians offers us a helpful guide for how we might do so. Writing to that strategic church, Paul tells them in chapter 4, "Let your conversation always be full of grace, seasoned with salt, so that you may know how to answer everyone." Salt adds taste to what it is used on. Therefore, when we season our conversation with salt, we ensure that our words will be tasteful.

But even more important is Paul's emphasis on grace. "Let your conversation *always* be full of grace." In other words, if in everything we are certain that our words will cast favor on their recipients, then we won't have to worry about how others will hear them. If we live in grace and think in grace, then what we say and do will always exude it.

I know in my own life there have been times when someone caught me off guard and, after the fact, I thought about what I might have said in response to them. And usually, what I wish I had said was not anything graceful or tasteful. So, maybe I was better off not saying anything. Or maybe, instead of silence, if my heart had been more full of grace, then I could have said something that might have better eased any tension that had been in the air.

If grace abounds in us, then grace will flow through us—the same grace that come to us through our faith in Jesus. Today, be a party to grace and then you will seize every opportunity that comes your way to advance the cause of Christ and be the salt of the earth he desires all his disciples to be.

No Need to Be Afraid

2 Samuel 6:6-12

When they came to the threshing floor of Nakon, Uzzah reached out and took hold of the ark of God, because the oxen stumbled. The LORD's anger burned against Uzzah because of his irreverent act; therefore God struck him down, and he died there beside the ark of God.

Like many people my age, I grew up with a notion of God that caused me to fear him more than to embrace him. I don't mean to be disrespectful to all those who taught me about God during my growing-up years. They had been taught the same thing. But as I look at Scripture today, I see increasingly how our approach to God must be based more on wonder than pure fear and a willingness to yield ourselves to his sovereign will, grateful all the while that when we do, God favors us in the most remarkable ways.

Evidently, people have always struggled with learning how to reverence God while not allowing their reverence to drive them to dread him. In 2 Samuel 6, we see this struggle even in King David, a man after God's own heart according to the Scriptures. David has instructed his men to go with him to Baalah, to the house of Abinidab, to bring the ark from there to his capital in Jerusalem. Two of the sons of Abinidab, Uzzah and Ahio, are guiding the cart that bears the ark when the cart hits a bump in the road and looks as if it will turn over. And when Uzzah reaches out to secure the ark, the LORD's anger burns against Uzzah for what Scripture calls an irreverent act, and Uzzah dies on the spot.

Now, there's a lot going on in this story. More than likely, Uzzah's familiarity with the ark, having seen in it in his father's house, led him to take its sanctity for granted. Maybe the story is designed to tell us that God is capable of taking care of himself and doesn't need our help. Most assuredly, it tells us that when we reverence God in the most appropriate ways, we do not need to fear God; as we instead reverence him, God responds with immeasurable blessing.

How do you relate to God? If you are dreadfully afraid of God, thinking that God is about to smite you at any moment, think again. The cross of Jesus is all the proof you need that God loves you and will go to any extent to reconcile you, sinner that you are, to him. With the LORD there is inexhaustible mercy. But on the other hand, if you presume upon God's grace, if you take God for granted, know there are consequences for such a cavalier attitude. The God who gave you life deserves more than your nonchalance; God deserves your devotion, your wonder, and your respect. That middle ground between fear and presumption is where true reverence lies, and manifold blessings that come from it. Stay in that place today and you will see that with God you have nothing to fear. You have everything to gain, as you order your whole life in God's direction, just as Jesus taught—in Spirit and in truth.

All That God Gives

Psalm 68:35

You, God, are awesome in your sanctuary;
the God of Israel gives power and strength to his people.

Where do you get your (fill in the blank)? Your patience, your personality, your perseverance? Some people get asked a question such as that when they seem to possess a rare ability that few others own. And the people who ask the question are wondering if it might be possible for them to have it too.

For people of faith, we confess that as the book of James tells us, "Every good and perfect gift comes from God." Just as life is a gift from God, so are the talents and abilities that enable us to fulfill God's purpose in life. And if for any moment we begin to think otherwise, we find ourselves with not nearly enough to accomplish whatever it is we are called upon to do.

No one understood that principle more than the Psalmist. Since many of the Psalms are attributed to David, we can overlay those promises expressed in them with David's life. David, for example, was a shepherd boy who won the day against Goliath, the Philistine giant. And not only did David defeat Goliath; but he also defeated all of his enemies who dared to stand in his way, because in truth they were standing in God's way. And in Psalm 68, David invites the people to join him in praising God, who is the source of not only his help, but also the nation's help. "You, God," says the Psalmist, "are awesome in your sanctuary; the God of Israel gives power and strength to his people." The God who reigns on high in glory condescends to mortal people to empower them for the purpose of doing his will.

Such is the message of the gospel; is it not? God came down in the person of Jesus to do for us what we could not do for ourselves. And as Jesus ascended into heaven, the Holy Spirit descended upon the church so that they might be filled with power, as the book of Acts puts it, "so that they could be witnesses to the ends of the earth."

Today, welcome that power into your own life. Find God's strength for the challenges you have to face. And when others see you overcoming all that comes against you, they'll possibly ask where you get such power and strength. Be ready to tell them: because God wills for everyone to know Jesus and the life more abundant that only he can make possible.

Wisdom Is Proved Right

Luke 7:35

But wisdom is proved right by all her children.

Wisdom is a most important topic in the Bible. Both Old and New Testaments contain passages that tout its virtues. More than mere intellectual knowledge, wisdom is the ability that God calls all of us to possess where we discern his truth and then we apply it to everyday life.

In Luke 7, Jesus has affirmed the ministry of John the Baptist, the forerunner to the Messiah. Many who had gathered nodded their heads and hearts in affirmation of what Jesus was saying, especially since most of them, including the tax collectors Luke tells us, had been baptized by John in the wilderness. In fact, the only group who balked about Jesus' words were the very people who should have accepted them the most, the Pharisees and teachers of the law, who had refused John's baptism of repentance because they had thought they didn't need it.

Jesus saw he couldn't win for losing with these religious experts who thought themselves holier than others. "What can I say? John the Baptist didn't drink wine and often fasted and you say he was possessed with a demon. Meanwhile, the Son of Man feasts and drinks and you call him a glutton and drunkard and a friend of sinners, the worst kind." But sizing up the situation, Jesus came to this conclusion: "But wisdom is proved right by her children." In other words, those who live God's truth, whether they do without or choose to celebrate, show their true colors by the way they honor God's commandments in deeds and not words. They are wise enough to see that although John and Jesus went about honoring God in very different ways, their goal was the same: to call people back to God, not to turn them away as did the Pharisees and teachers of the Law.

How do your words and deeds influence others? Do they drive people to God, or do they drive them away? Do they encourage repentance and faith, or do they create doubt? The wise among us will always consider how we promote God's purposes and not our own. Our faithfulness will show people that we belong to God, we are his children, and there's plenty of room for any who will join us in God's way.

What God Will Never Do

Psalm 89:32-33

I will punish their sin with the rod, their iniquity with flogging;
but I will not take my love from him, nor will I ever betray my faithfulness.

How much in this life can you really count on? We've all experienced letdowns in terms of people we thought we could trust, only to find out that their trust was conditional.

I don't say this to discourage you, but instead to point you to One who will never disappoint. I'm talking of course about God. Sometimes we think that God's anger toward our sin causes him to be conditional in his support of us, but that is not so. Yes, God expects and even demands that we do what he gives us to do. And when we fail to do so, there are consequences to our rebellion. But those consequences never diminish the deep devotion God has toward us and the manner in which God will always be working in our best interest.

In Psalm 89, the Psalmist reflects upon this part of God's nature. God has made a promise to David that one of David's sons will always reign on the throne of Israel. And yes, there are warnings as to the calamities that would take place if any of those sons decided to lead the people out of his own will instead of God's. But the Psalmist makes this confession, speaking to the people in God's voice: "But I will not take my love from him, nor will I ever betray my faithfulness." The one thing God cannot do, the Bible tells us, is to go back on his word. We can always count on God.

I hope your day goes exceedingly well. But many days, they don't. Something happens to discourage and disappoint us. Someone doesn't come through for us, someone we were counting on to do so. We're all human. At times we, too, let others down. But the one constant in life is God. God cannot betray his faithfulness, and God's love for us abounds forever. Let that love well up in you and flow through you so that you also will be someone others can count on; so that as one who works for the well-being of others, you will be known as a peacemaker, and as Jesus said, you will become a child of God.

Meeting People Where They Are

Acts 17:22-23

Paul then stood up in the meeting of the Areopagus and said: "People of Athens! I see that in every way you are very religious. For as I walked around and looked carefully at your objects of worship, I even found an altar with this inscription: To an unknown GOD. So you are ignorant of the very thing you worship—and this is what I am going to proclaim to you.

One of the most famous sermons in the Bible is the one Paul preached in Athens at Mars Hill. We read about Paul's experience in Acts 17. Paul has arrived at this intellectual center of the first-century world and while he waits on Silas and Timothy to come from Berea, he takes a look around the city and becomes distressed that it is so filled with idols. Paul then goes to the Areopagus, the place where daily debates are held, and there he takes on the intellectuals of his day. But notice how Paul does so. He looks for a point of connection, telling his audience, "I can see that in every way you are religious. You even have an altar with an inscription to an Unknown God." Paul then begins to help them know the God and Father of our LORD Jesus Christ, the one true God who gives life to all who trust in him.

What makes Paul's message so controversial to many people today is how they focus on the fact that some of the intellectuals at the Areopagus sneered at Paul, and so they contend that Paul failed in his proclamation of the gospel. But what those critics fail to consider is that the text also tells us that some of the intellectuals wanted to hear more about Paul's message of resurrection and there were some who actually believed, including a man named Dionysius and a woman named Damaris, named in the text no doubt because they surely became leaders in the church that came into being in Athens.

The point is that it makes good sense for us today, living as we do in a world where we can no longer count on people being familiar with the stories of Scripture, to meet people where they are. Start with listening to their beliefs. Pause to consider the values that drive them. Then pray for the Holy Spirit to help you connect the good news of Jesus with their beliefs and values, helping them to see how Jesus fulfills what they still are lacking. I call it "scratching their itch," and everyone has some kind of itch when it comes to what really matters in life.

Yes, some people may scoff and others may sneer. If that happened to Paul at Mars Hill, it will likely happen to us. But some will want to have more conversation, and better yet, some will believe. One thing is for certain: as the prophet Isaiah reminds us, God's Word never returns to him null or void. It accomplishes everything God purposes for it to do. Trust in that promise and meet people with the gospel. Then those who are itching to know the truth will find the answers for which they yearn, and the joy and peace that come from knowing Jesus and the life such knowledge alone makes possible.

Lead Me Higher

Psalm 61:1-3

Hear my cry, O God; listen to my prayer.
From the ends of the earth I call to you, I call as my heart grows faint;
lead me to the rock that is higher than I.
For you have been my refuge, a strong tower against the foe.

Like many people, I am scared of heights. Still, I'm not scared enough that I don't appreciate a higher perspective, one that allows me to take in what I can't see at eye level. I don't know why this is so. Perhaps it's just that I'm more confident when my feet are planted on firm ground.

I've heard that all babies are born with the fear of falling. That makes sense to me. In the course of life there are more than enough situations that knock the props out from under us, so we seem most at peace when we don't have to worry about having to take such a tumble. But what if we could have a higher perspective and at the same time know the assurance that having our feet under us provides?

In Psalm 61, the Psalmist invokes God's presence and power to find such assurance. He sees on the horizon challenges that threaten to knock him down and cause him to fall, and he knows how in his own power he won't be able to get back up. So, instead of facing these challenges on his own, the Psalmist calls upon God. He asks God specifically to hear his cry and, in his words, to "lead me to the rock that is higher than I." The Psalmist knew that most battles are won by the party that secures the high ground, and with God, the "King of the Mountain" on your side, what challenge can come against you?

If you find yourself feeling wobbly and uncertain because of some challenge that is before you, call on God for help. God will hear your cry and lift you from your distress and assure you of his abiding presence. Then you will be at a place where you can see that with God, all things are possible; you can be more than a conqueror through him who loved you and has promised that nothing will separate you from his love for you in Christ Jesus.

Complete Your Task

Acts 20:24

However, I consider my life worth nothing to me;
my only aim is to finish the race and complete the task the LORD Jesus has given me
—the task of testifying to the good news of God's grace.

Many people are good at starting things. They come up with ideas and start out implementing them with great enthusiasm. But then they come across bumps in the road and rough patches that slow them down. And if they're not careful, they never finish what they began.

Nothing satisfies a soul more than to see something through to its completion. And never is this more true than with matters of faith.

In Acts 20, Paul is leaving Miletus, a coastal city in Asia Minor, or modern-day Turkey. He is going back to Jerusalem where he senses in his spirit that there will challenges awaiting him in the Holy City. So, he calls the elders from the church in Ephesus to come to see him off. It is a teary goodbye. Paul, after all, has stayed in Ephesus, much longer than any other place he preached. And as Paul explains the burden in his heart, he says to the elders, "I consider my life worth nothing to me. My only aim is to complete the task the LORD Jesus has given me." And with that, Paul tells them goodbye and heads off to Jerusalem to finish what God has given him to do.

Yes, Paul went off from Miletus with deep emotion, but he also set off with great resolve. Paul's life was marked by obedience to the Spirit, and nothing could lift his heart more than following through on God's purpose for his life.

Why is it that so many people today are good at starting something but not so good at finishing it? There are many reasons: They have too much on their plates. They have too many loyalties and commitments. They focus on themselves and what is comfortable and convenient. No wonder people are so scattered today. If we have in our hearts a compelling sense of what we are to do with our lives, then we will be able to overcome all of the forces that want to stop us from doing it. And if "the what" is governed by Jesus, there is nothing that can stand in our way.

You've got a lot you likely need to take care of today; so do I. But let's make sure none of it rises above what Jesus gives us to do. If we keep our main focus on Jesus' calling, then no sadness, no setbacks, no selfish motivations will stop us in our tracks.

What's the old saying? "The main thing is to keep the main thing the main thing." If the main thing is what Jesus has given you to do, you won't so much worry about how to keep it as you will come to see the marvelous manner in which it will always be keeping you.

Remembering Who You Are

Psalm 61:5

For you, God, have heard my vows;
you have given me the heritage of those who fear your name.

The loss of one's memory must be a terrible thing. Oh, I know that all of us have some memories we'd like to erase, but my guess is that most of us have far more good memories that we'd never want to forget, good memories that sustain us when storm clouds arise and things get shaky in life.

The best memory of all is knowing who you are and keeping that knowledge at the forefront of your heart. Many of us can remember when we were young that our parents would send us off with the admonition, "Now, you remember who you are." It was their way of reminding us that we should not let our foolish impulses get the best of us and bring shame to the family name

Sadly, there are some people who never come to that self-knowledge. And as a result, they live aimlessly, without purpose. The famous mythologist of the last century, Joseph Campbell, called such a life a "wasteland life." Now, that's a vivid image.

But when you look at the Bible, you see how emphasis is placed on developing this self-knowledge so that along life's way you'll act wisely and faithfully. In the Old Testament, families were responsible for handing down their traditions from generation to generation through ritual observances such as Passover. And in the New Testament, Jesus instituted what we call the LORD's Supper to serve as a memorial meal. "Do this in remembrance of me." It was Jesus' way of teaching us that we find our true identity in him.

Psalm 61:5 has the Psalmist proclaiming: "For you, God, have heard my vows; you have given me the heritage of those who fear your name." The Psalmist recognized that knowing who you are isn't knowledge you acquire or attain on your own. It's a gift. Just as you are born into a family, biologically speaking, you are born into a family spiritually speaking. We evangelicals call that being "born again," or being "born from above."

You are a child of God, a co-heir of God's through Jesus Christ. God has spared no expense reconciling you unto himself. As you go about your daily activities, hold on to that heritage and let it drive everything you say and do. Then you will be careful not to bring any shame upon God's family.

Content in Every Situation

Philippians 4:12-13

I know what it is to be in need, and I know what it is to have plenty. I have learned the secret of being content in any and every situation, whether well fed or hungry, whether living in plenty or in want. I can do all this through him who gives me strength.

Some people are not easily pleased, and others never are. Needless to say, having to deal with those sorts of people tries our patience and taxes our resolve, even though the problem lies not with us.

If you are a soul who finds it hard to be satisfied, perhaps the root of your problem lies with the fact that you haven't yet leaned sufficiently on the strength that Jesus provides.

No doubt the most famous verse in the book of Philippians is this: "I can do all things through Christ who gives me strength" (4:13). Most of us take that verse as a sort of mantra for finding the power we need to overcome all challenges that come our way, but that's not really what Paul meant. Look at the verse before it, the one where Paul says that he has learned how to be content in every circumstance and situation. The key, he writes, is by learning to lean on Christ's strength, not his own. How is it that we've missed this deep connection between our contentment and the strength that faith in Jesus provides us?

I'm not suggesting that faith in Jesus won't see you through challenging situations, but there are better verses to lean on to make that claim. I am suggesting that if you ever find it hard to be at peace with your situation, maybe the answer lies with trusting in Jesus.

When you become empty or drained or dissatisfied with your lot in life, focus more intently on Jesus. Look to him to fill that void in your soul. Let your heart rest in the peace he provides. Then you won't be a person others feel the need to avoid. You'll be a witness to Jesus' provision and the abiding contentment his presence in you always makes possible.

The LORD Laughs at the Wicked

Psalm 37:12-13

The wicked plot against the righteous and gnash their teeth at them;
but the LORD laughs at the wicked, for he knows their day is coming.

"That's no laughing matter." You've probably heard someone say that or perhaps you've said it yourself when a situation has become so serious that someone feels the need to laugh to lessen the tension. Laughter can be an ego defense mechanism, a way to slough something off as if it poses no threat, when the fact of the matter is that it really does.

Wickedness would fall into that category; wouldn't you say? Wickedness is something I can't imagine anyone laughing at. And yet, in Psalm 37:13, we hear the Psalmist say: "the LORD laughs at the wicked, for he knows their day is coming."

The reason God laughs is not because God is trying to take the air out of a tense situation, nor because God minimizes the evil, nor because God feels threatened in any way. It's the case that God know how everything will play out, and in his sovereign power God knows that nothing will stand in the way of him accomplishing Kingdom purposes. And so, when God laughs at the wickedness that exists in our world, he does so because he knows that it has a short shelf life.

I'm not suggesting that you laugh at the wickedness that may come your way today. You're not God; neither am I. But I am suggesting that you consider how that wickedness poses no threat to God's purposes in your life. You know that because of your faith in the Risen Jesus, over whom death could not even hold sway. Know that its days are numbered and your days are not. Then may the laughter that you hear in the distance encourage you and bring you joy, knowing that nothing will ever separate you from God's love in Jesus Christ. Your life, even in the face of the most pronounced wickedness, is forever secure.

Better the Little

Psalm 37:16-17

Better the little that the righteous have than the wealth of many wicked;
for the power of the wicked will be broken,
but the LORD upholds the righteous.

We live in a world where most people believe that the more you have the better off you are. But is that a fact? Are the people with the biggest bank accounts, largest houses, and greatest toys and gadgets really in a good place in life? Sometimes the upkeep on all of those material goods creates levels of anxiety that few of us would want to manage. It's a reminder that the best life isn't necessarily one that can be easily quantified. Instead, it is qualitative and only measured by the joy and peace one feels within.

A good number of the Psalms are worship poems that God's people employed to connect their faith to everyday life. Even back then, people were prone to compare themselves by how their possessions stacked up against others. And when those comparisons were made against nations that did not follow God, it was easy for God's people to wonder if they had made the right choice. Psalm 37 assures them they did: "Better the little the righteous have than the wealth of many wicked, for the power of the wicked will be broken, but the LORD upholds the righteous." The power of the wicked will be broken: that's future tense. The wicked may seem to be prospering today, but that won't last forever. Meanwhile, the LORD upholds the righteous: that's present tense. Even now God has those who trust in him under his providential care. And how much is that worth?

That's a good question for you to ask today as you go about your everyday activities. Whether you have much or little, if you have the assurance that God abides with you, you have everything you need.

Where God Leads

Genesis 46:2-4

And God spoke to Israel in a vision at night and said, "Jacob! Jacob!" "Here I am," he replied. "I am God, the God of your father," he said. "Do not be afraid to go down to Egypt, for I will make you into a great nation there. I will go down to Egypt with you, and I will surely bring you back again. And Joseph's own hand will close your eyes."

Some years ago, when I was planning a group trip to the Holy Land, I was somewhat surprised by the number of people who told me, "I'd be too afraid to go there." I know there are safer places to be today than in the Middle East, but I also know that if you were to turn on the evening news in any major city in America on any day—including the one you call home—you'd think there wasn't a more dangerous place on the planet. The point is that we find a way to overcome our fears to be in a place where we feel we belong.

In Genesis 46, God tells Jacob not to be afraid to go into Egypt, a foreign country from his homeland of Canaan. Jacob, however, had just learned that Joseph, his son whom he thought he had lost years ago, was in fact alive and he was begging his father and the entire family to come to him in Egypt.

To Jacob's credit, he didn't let his love for his son get in the way of his obedience to God. So, before he packed anything, he prayed to God, who said to Jacob, "Don't be afraid to go down to Egypt, for I will make you a great nation and bring you back again." Only then did Jacob go, knowing the hand of God was upon him.

Today, God may be directing you along a path that may seem too good to be true—so much so that you are reluctant to take it because you think it may be your heart telling you to go and not God. But if you pray about it and God still gives you the go-ahead, then take it in peace and in promise.

Those who trust their way to God will never have to live in fear. God will be with them to protect them, to bless them, and to provide for them every step of the way. May today you find God doing all of that for you. Then every step you take will be on land you can call holy.

Hold Fast

Joshua 23:6-8

Be very strong; be careful to obey all that is written in the Book of the Law of Moses, without turning aside to the right or to the left. Do not associate with these nations that remain among you; do not invoke the names of their gods or swear by them. You must not serve them or bow down to them. But you are to hold fast to the LORD your God, as you have until now.

Have you ever cherished something so much that you found yourself clutching it so close to your heart that you would never think of letting it get out of your sight? That's the sure test of how important something or someone is to you. We order our lives around whatever is close to our heart and define our sense of worth by it.

In the book of Joshua, which is the story of Israel's conquest of the promised land of Canaan, the Hebrews have been led by Joshua, the successor to Moses. The time has come for Joshua to depart the scene, and he, as did Moses, gathers the people for a farewell address. In that address Joshua emphasizes the importance of Israel's need to stay ever close to God, as their failure to do so would jeopardize all that God has done for them.

In chapter 23, as Joshua is challenging the elders of the 12 tribes, he offers them this reminder: "Hold fast to the LORD your God, as you have until now." If there seems to have been a hint of doubt in Joshua's voice, there most likely was. After all, Joshua had seen too many instances of the people's failure to obey God's direction. He knew there was no guarantee that such a pattern would not carry on without due commitment from the nation's leaders. But Joshua was certain of God's steadfastness. While the people wouldn't always be found faithful before God, God would always be faithful to them. And therein would they find their hope for tomorrow.

The same truth applies to us today. We're not always constant. We are strong in our faith one day and much weaker the next. But God is ever constant. God's love in Jesus Christ is steadfast and sure. Hold that love close to your heart today: it will sustain you whatever comes your way, and you can look to your future with all the confidence that it will be all you would want it to be, and even more.

God Doesn't Always Agree

Psalm 50:21

When you did these things and I kept silent,
you thought I was exactly like you.
But I now arraign you and set my accusations before you.

One of the benefits of prayer is that it enables us to get on the same page as God about matters in life. When we're not in sync with God, it's not God's fault. God's will is good, acceptable, and perfect, as Paul writes in Romans 12. And because our hearts' desire is rarely that, we have a disconnect, one that can only be resolved through open and earnest prayer.

We see that type of prayer in many of the Psalms. In Psalm 50, the Psalmist shows us how such prayer is not a trifling thing. Honest engagement with God comes at a cost. We must be ready for God to confront us with all that is sideways in us; only then can God's mercy make us right.

In the first part Psalm 50, the Psalmist is God's mouthpiece, explaining to the wicked how they find it easy to spout pious phrases despite their sinful ways because of their assumption that God sees things as they do. But God helps them see otherwise. In verse 21, God counters their assumption in this way: "When you did these things (these inexcusable transgressions) and I kept silent, you thought I was exactly like you. But now I arraign you and set my accusations before you." In other words, like a prosecuting attorney, God offered a case that far from his silence being tacit agreement, it was more a choice on God's part to wait until the right time to confront his people with their sinful ways. God did not want to cast them off. But God knew his people would not be able to hear the truth until they had come to a place where their sins would find them out.

Don't get to such a place today. Don't assume that God sees everything and everyone as you. Don't interpret God's silence in your circumstances as his approval. Instead, live prayerfully and openly. Be earnest in your desire to align your heart with God's. Only then can God's ways truly become your ways and his truth in Jesus Christ fully set you free.

You Are a Part

1 Corinthians 12:27

Now you are the body of Christ,
and each one of you is a part of it.

One of the most beautiful ways the New Testament describes the church is the way it speaks of it as the body of Christ. That was Paul's metaphor, which he passed on to the church at Corinth, the last church you'd ever think would have merited such a description. The Corinthian church was torn by factions and jealousies, power plays and immoralities. Someone has said that there is no problem a church might face today that wasn't faced already by the church at Corinth. And yet because Jesus hadn't given up on those believers, Paul couldn't give up on them either. And so, in 1 Corinthians 12, Paul tells the church: "Now you are the body of Christ, and each one of you is a part of it."

Everyone has a place in the church, and everyone has a role. We don't all have the same gifts or abilities. But each of us has something to offer, not because of who we are but because of the grace that has come to us through our faith in Christ. That's the meaning of the word "charisma." Charisma literally means "grace gift." And each believer in Jesus has some expression of it to employ.

None of us is perfect, but all of us are loved and cherished. Accept that gift today so that it might awaken in you something you can offer for the church's witness to Jesus. This world needs a witness that will turn it away from the false narratives of despair all around to the hope of the gospel. You are a part of the body of Christ, so do your part. Use your gift wisely and, more importantly, use it faithfully. Then the church will better live into the purpose God has for it, which is simply to mediate the presence of Christ to a lost and dying world that others too might know his love that lifts us up and provides grace sufficient for our every need.

Trust Every Need to Jesus

Mark 8:4

His disciples answered,
"But where in this remote place can anyone get enough bread to feed them?"

No life is problem-free. Sometimes we may think that people who trust in Jesus have all their problems magically removed, but that is not so. If anything, we might argue that people who follow Jesus bring upon themselves even more challenges.

So, why follow Jesus? We follow Jesus because of what he brings to bear against all problems. In him we find all that we need to solve our problems and overcome our challenges. While that's certainly not by itself how we should view our faith in Christ, it most definitely strengthens our spirits when problems come our way.

In the gospel of Mark, Jesus breaks into his world as the Son of God. Throughout Mark, Jesus goes from one challenging situation to the next, bringing to bear the power of God upon every one of them.

In Mark 8, a crowd has gathered to hear Jesus teach, but they have nothing to eat. Jesus has compassion on them, knowing they have been with him three days (a sacred number in the Bible), and he does not want to send them away hungry. But when he asks his disciples to help, they pass the buck. "Where in this remote place can anyone get enough bread to feed them?" Anyone? Their faith in Jesus is not yet what it should be. Then Jesus takes what they make available to him and multiplies it, and satisfies the crowd of 4,000 who have come to hear him.

The disciples had allowed the challenge to overwhelm them. But let's not be too hard on the disciples. So do we. We often let the challenges and problems in this life overwhelm us. But if we trusted those things to Jesus, what difference do you think it would make?

Your answer to that question will be a good measure of your faith. So, today, show the depth of your faith by not allowing your problems to get the best of you. Instead, let Jesus get the best of you. When you make your life available to him, you will see the great thing that Jesus can do. Your faith will be strengthened. And in the process, your problems will pale in the light of his glory and grace.

Don't Convict Yourself

2 Samuel 14:13

The woman said, "Why then have you devised a thing like this against the people of God? When the king says this, does he not convict himself, for the king has not brought back his banished son?"

The very definition of hypocrisy is to confess one thing but do another. Little wonder that the Bible speaks so forcefully against hypocrisy. God's cause never gets traction where such disingenuous behavior exists.

All of us are prone to hypocritical acts from time to time, even the most faithful of us. But what distinguishes faithful people from faithless ones is the willingness of the devoted to own up to their hypocrisy, confess it, and do whatever is necessary to bring the scales of justice back into balance.

In 2 Samuel 14, we read how King David was made aware of hypocrisy in his own heart and how he moved quickly to correct it. David's family, as we read in Scripture, wasn't the most functional family in his day. There was intrigue, jealousy, and outright abuse. For example, one of David's sons, Amnon, had violated his half-sister, Tamar. When her brother Absalom avenged his sister's shame by killing his brother, Absalom fled from the land knowing that his father's wrath would fall upon him. Thus, David's house was divided.

But Joab, commander of David's army, devised a plan to bring Absalom home. He employed a wise woman from the land of Tekoa to tell a sad story of her own household that had become divided by internal animosity. When this woman shared her story with David, he assured her that no harm would fall upon her son who had taken out his own anger against his brother in the same way that Absalom had done against Amnon. After the king's assurances, the woman then asked David why he could not do the same thing with his own son: "Why have you devised a thing like this against the people of God? When the king says this, does he not convict himself, for the king has not brought back his banished son?" The woman's story had made David see that his house was in disarray because he had taken matters into his own hands instead of trusting the dysfunction to God.

Therein lies the root of all hypocrisy. Hypocrites can't trust their circumstances to God. They insist on being in control of everything, when the truth is they can control nothing. Isn't this the charge Jesus leveled against the religious rulers of his day who couldn't believe God was fulfilling his redemptive purposes in Jesus?

Don't let dysfunction abound in any area of your life by fueling it with your desire to wrest control of the situation from God. Trust in God and see God's grace at work in ways the assure you that your future will be blessed. Then instead of convicting yourself, you will be leaning upon God's everlasting arms, arms that will keep you safe and secure from all life's alarms, which is the best evidence of a functional life and a functional faith.

Have a Minute?

Fulfill the Law of Christ

Galatians 6:2

Carry each other's burdens,
and in this way you will fulfill the law of Christ.

Law is a religious concept that we don't see applying to Christian faith, at least not after the sacrifice Jesus made on the cross to free us from the burden of shouldering it. Granted, the new covenant Jesus established is one based on God's unconditional grace toward us sinners, which we appropriate through our faith in his son.

But grace doesn't mean that we are free of responsibilities to take on. It's just that we don't take them on to be put right with God; we take them on because we have already been put right with God by grace through faith in Jesus. Or as I like to say, we don't do good works in order to be saved; we do them because we have been saved.

Paul wrote his letter to the Galatians precisely to counter the false teachings of the Judaizers, a group of Christians who were trying to encourage Gentile converts to trust Jesus and follow the law of Moses. The burden of following the commandments were too much for these new Christians, so Paul saw the need to write to them and explain that saving faith is devotion to Jesus alone. It's not Jesus plus anything.

Yet Paul also recognized the importance of living such faith. In Galatians 6, he invites his readers to support one another in this way: "Carry each other's burdens, and in this way you fulfill the law of Christ." I find Paul's use of "law" most interesting. No doubt, he intended it to be a not-so-subtle dig at his opponents, who were obsessed with evidence of their devotion. Paul counseled, "If you want to prove your faith, help others. Then, you will be living in the spirit of Jesus, who carried our burdens with him to the cross."

You may know of someone who is struggling under a weight of shame or insecurity or loneliness or a thousand other loads. Your salvation won't be helped or hurt by ignoring them and their pain, but their salvation very well could be. A word of understanding, a listening shoulder, or a helping hand on your part can be the grace they need to move beyond whatever weight of the world may be keeping them from the abundance Jesus wants them to know. Equally importantly, it may also be the way for you to know such abundance as through your gracious love you come to fulfill the law of Christ.

Find Out What Pleases the LORD

Ephesians 5:8-10

For you were once darkness, but now you are light in the LORD.
Live as children of light
(for the fruit of the light consists in all goodness, righteousness and truth)
and find out what pleases the LORD.

How do you give something to someone who has everything? That's a dilemma we face from time to time when a special occasion draws near and we have to come up with a gift for someone who seems impossible to buy for. When such an occasion arises, we do one of two things: We either go with our instincts or we ask the person what she wants. Usually, neither of those responses rises to the occasion, and we end up consoling ourselves with the notion that perhaps the other person will be satisfied with knowing it's the thought that counts.

But have you stopped to consider how there might be a third option? We could lean more deeply into our relationship with that person, and therefore become so in tune with her heart that it becomes clear what she wants more than anything else.

In Ephesians 5, the Apostle Paul commends that approach when it comes to our relationship with the LORD. Talk about someone hard to give to: What do you give a God who has everything and in Jesus gave his all to us? If Paul can be believed, that question is not as hard to answer as you might think. He writes, "Live as children of light...and find out what pleases the LORD." In other words, in the course of our obedience we come to see how in tune our hearts are with the LORD's heart so that everything we say and do pleases him, whom we owe so much.

Today, think about this truth as you go about your daily activities. Make sure that every moment you are aware of how your behavior reflects the light of Christ and does not serve the darkness. Show the changes that your faith in Jesus has brought about. Then, God will be pleased, the cause of Christ will be furthered, and your heart will be filled with joy, because while the thought counts, so do our words and deeds. They all work together in ways that please our LORD to no end.

Take Refuge in God's Mercy

Psalm 57:1

Have mercy on me, my God,
have mercy on me, for in you I take refuge.
I will take refuge in the shadow of your wings until the disaster has passed.

Life's storms are inevitable, both meteorologically speaking and spiritually speaking. Just as we can't avoid those summer thunder bursts that come seemingly every afternoon, neither can we avoid those calamitous times that test our patience and faith.

It seems like the last year or more has been one giant test of our faith, as we've had to quarantine, mask up, be set free, go out and about, only to be at a point where it seems that COVID variants are about to start the cycle all over again. How does a person keep his mind? Actually, the better question is, "How does a person keep his heart?"

According to the Psalmist, you don't. You let God keep it instead. Psalm 57 is a cry for mercy in which the Psalmist begins with these words: "Have mercy on me, God. Have mercy on me, for in you I take refuge. I will take refuge in the shadow of your wings until the disaster has passed."

Every disaster passes, though few pass as quickly as we'd like. But what stays with us is God's presence and God's protection. No calamity can bring that into question.

So, today, find shelter in the face of all calamities by embracing God's promised protection. Let God keep your mind and your heart so that you might love him with all your mind and heart. Then you will once again be walking in the way of Jesus, who trusted his calamity to the Father and experienced not only God's presence and protection, but also his resurrection power. Know that God's mercy will save this day, and every day that lies ahead.

The Assurance Jesus Gives

John 6:39-40

And this is the will of him who sent me, that I shall lose none of all those he has given me, but raise them up at the last day. For my Father's will is that everyone who looks to the Son and believes in him shall have eternal life, and I will raise them up at the last day.

People speak of faith in terms of probabilities, and rightly so. There is always an element of uncertainty inherent to faith; otherwise, there wouldn't be any need to risk everything for Jesus.

And yet there is also a sense of assurance that comes to people of faith, which is different from certainty. Everyone wants to know that the chair they sit down in will hold them up, but they don't know until they actually plant themselves down into it. And once they do, they become confident that the chair will keep them off the floor. It's the act of commitment that results in the assurance.

In John 6, Jesus has just offered another one of his "I Am" sayings in which he lays claim to God's authority in his own life. "I am the Bread of Life," he tells the crowds who had ventured to the other side of the Sea of Galilee to find him after he had fed 5,000 of them. "Whoever comes to me will never go hungry and whoever believes in me will never be thirsty." That's assurance.

And then to double down on his promise, Jesus declares to them that the ground for such assurance lies with his connection to the Father. "For my Father's will is that everyone who looks to the Son and believes in him will have eternal life, and I will raise them up on the last day."

Life is rife with uncertainty. There is little if anything you can count on in everyday experience. And though faith has its share of ambiguity and vagueness, if it's fixed on Jesus, he promises to work in you in ways that give you the confidence that in due time everything will become more clear.

Your life with Jesus is in good hands, hands that will hold you and never let you fall. Whatever your need, Jesus can meet; and in the grand scheme of things, surely you can live with that.

Your Family Resemblance

Acts 6:15

All who were sitting in the Sanhedrin looked intently at Stephen,
and they saw that his face was like the face of an angel.

The older I get, the more people say I look like my father. And the older my son gets, the more people say the same to him. That stands to reason, does it not? Family resemblances derive from those genes that get passed down from generation to generation.

So, do people recognize your family resemblance that comes from your faith? That stands to reason as well. After all, the Bible tells us early on that each of us was created in the image of God (Gen. 1:27) and that the goal of our redemption is to conform to the image of Christ (Rom. 8:29). If people can't see evidence that we have been with Jesus, we need to question our devotion.

The book of Acts tells the story of Stephen, the first martyr of Christianity. In chapter 6, where after having been chosen as one of the first "deacons" of the early church, Stephen goes out and contends for the faith in incontrovertibly wise ways. His prowess in proclaiming Jesus results in stiff opposition and scurrilous charges. But when Stephen is brought before the Sanhedrin, the ruling council of the religious authorities, they cannot deny his family resemblance. The text tells us: "They saw that his face was like the face of an angel."

The word angel means "messenger." Even Stephen's opponents could see that his words weren't merely his own; they were imbued with divine wisdom.

As you go about your activities today, I trust people will be able to say the same of you. They can if, like Stephen, you fill your soul with the wisdom from on high. Then, regardless of whatever conflict or dissension you may encounter, while others may not agree with you on everything, they won't be able to counter your heart. The family resemblance will be too hard to deny. As the hymn encourages us, "Keep telling the story. Be faithful and true. Let others see Jesus in you."

Crushing Satan, Bestowing Peace

Romans 16:20

The God of peace will soon crush Satan under your feet.
The grace of our LORD Jesus be with you.

No one needs to be convinced that evil exists in the most profound forms. Even worse, it's impossible to think that any of us can always avoid it. Evil rears its ugly head when we least expect it, and does so in the most deceptive forms. As the psychiatrist Scott Peck reminded us in his *People of the Lie*, evil people tend to hide behind the façade of good and do their greatest damage to others because of their refusal to confront the wrongdoing in their own hearts.

In Romans 16, Paul ends his great epistle by warning his readers to be on guard for those *from within their number* who serve their own interests instead of Christ's. In so doing, they also serve Satan's interests, the one who masquerades as an angel of light (2 Cor. 11:14). However, Paul assures his readers that these pawns of Satan will not stand in the way of the redemptive purposes God has made possible through their faith in Jesus. As Paul assures the church, the "God of peace will soon crush Satan under your feet. The grace of our LORD Jesus be with you." In other words, grace not only contains pardon for our own past evil; but it also contains power to overcome the evil that others, wittingly or unwittingly, bring our way.

I wish I could assure you that your faith in Christ will spare you from having to deal with evil in your everyday experience, but I can't. But I can assure you that such evil will not prevail. God's grace through your faith in Jesus will crush it, and in the meantime, it will keep you. God's grace will keep you in perfect peace because Jesus will be with you every step of your way.

The LORD Knows How to Rescue His Own

1 Peter 2:9

*If this is so, then the LORD knows how to rescue the godly from trials
and to hold the unrighteous for punishment on the day of judgment.*

Years ago, when I was in high school, I spent some of my summers as a lifeguard at local swimming pools. I had gone through Red Cross certification and had completed the requirements to attain a merit badge in Boy Scouts. But if put in a situation today where I had to pull someone out of the water, I don't know that I could do it. Some of the techniques I've forgotten, and even if I remembered them all, I'm not the same person in my 60s that I was at 16. Some of you can probably relate. And so, the chances are, if anyone ever needed a lifeguard while swimming, I'd be the last person they would turn to.

But let's take the matter away from swimming and on to where most of you are today. Knowing that you have a lifeguard you can count on each day, in the sense of someone who watches over you and looks after you, is an important thing. All of us find ourselves in places where we're in something that's deep and way over our heads, and at times we're not sure that we can make it on our own. When those times come, where do you turn for help?

In Peter's second letter, he encourages believers to look first to the LORD. As he writes in chapter 2, "the LORD knows how to rescues the godly from trials." The implication is that we can trust in him.

Today, you're likely to find yourself in a place where you'll need some outside help to get you through. Yes, you could turn to someone like yourself who has wisdom and power and financial resources. But don't neglect the help that Jesus provides. Jesus knows the trials you're going through, and he knows what it takes to see you through them. Most importantly, he has the power to do for you what you could never do for yourself. So, do what is necessary to grow in his grace and knowledge as you live boldly in his promise that he is watching over you every step of the way.

He Hears Our Cries

Psalm 28:6

Praise be to the LORD,
for he has heard my cry for mercy.

As a preacher, I'm always trying to tell if anyone out there in the congregation is paying attention. Trust me when I tell you that there's nothing worse than to be flapping your gums and have no one listening. Of course, I'll be quick to say that many of those times when I'm preaching and no one's listening, it's more my fault for not preaching better than it is the congregation's part for not listening better.

But you don't have to be a preacher to know how exasperating it is when you have something on your heart and you take the risk to express it, but no one seems interested in hearing you.

What if I were to tell you that there's one who is always ready to listen, one who bends in your direction and gives you his full attention? And what if I were to tell you that the someone is God?

In Psalm 28, the Psalmist offers his praise to God in the most effusive of ways because, as he puts it, "The LORD has heard my cry for mercy." No doubt the Psalmist had wasted his breath on some who let his words go in one ear and out the other. But God let the Psalmist's cries for mercies go straight to God's heart, where his response was to provide the Psalmist the strength he needed to rise above his difficulties.

God will the do the same for you, so don't hold back. Let God know your most pressing need. God will in no way turn a deaf ear to you. He will hear your cry for mercy and respond in kind so that your heart might leap for joy and your mouth give thanks to him in song.

How Much Do You Have?

Matthew 15:34

"How many loaves do you have?" Jesus asked.
"Seven," they replied, "and a few small fish."

My mother-in-law was hands down the best cook I have ever known. I've been blessed to have enjoyed a meal at many a table set by a most capable cook, but I have to say that my mother-in-law was consistently the best. That's because even if she wasn't expecting me, she could take what she had and whip up something that was absolutely scrumptious.

Taking what you have and doing a masterful job is what separates the amateur from the professional. But even if you don't consider yourself anything near an expert in anything, if you can make available to Jesus whatever is at your disposal, it's astounding what Jesus can do with it.

I'm thinking of course about the time that Jesus fed the multitudes with just seven loaves of bread and a few small fish. The crowd had gathered to hear Jesus teach and when it got late, Jesus didn't want them to send them away without something to eat. But when he asked his disciples what was at their disposal, their response was not promising: "Seven loaves. A few small fish. And what good will that do for a crowd such as this?"

What the disciples came to see was that Jesus can do remarkable things with seemingly miniscule resources, as long as people are willing to trust those resources to him.

We live in a world of great need. People are hurting everywhere, and they are especially hurting at this time. While you may be moved to do something about it, you may think that what you have is nowhere near what is necessary to have an impact. From a human perspective, it's probably not. But when Jesus gets his hands on it, all things are possible and all needs can be met.

Today when the opportunity presents itself to fill a hunger or thirst that presents itself to you, don't flinch. Have faith. Have faith in Jesus. His compassion moves him to do whatever is necessary to meet those needs. All that is required is a willing helper, a willing helper just like you.

Can Anyone Like This Be Found?

Genesis 41:37-38

The plan seemed good to Pharaoh and to all his officials.
So Pharaoh asked them,
"Can we find anyone like this man, one in whom is the spirit of God?"

The story of Joseph as told in Genesis tells of a life marked by more lows and highs than anyone I've ever known. But it ended on a high note to be sure, as Joseph found his way to a position of authority in Egypt. However, Joseph didn't get to that place by his own shrewdness or cunning. Joseph made it to the top because of how in every moment of his life, the LORD was with him.

In Genesis 41, Joseph has just emerged from prison to interpret Pharaoh's dreams, which pleased Pharaoh to no end. And as Pharaoh elevated Joseph from his prison to his palace, he did so for this reason: "Can we find anyone like this man, one in whom is the Spirit of God?"

How is it that people know you? What is your reputation? "Well, he's a wonderful conversation partner. She's a fantastic cook. She is a sharp as a tack. He is the best dressed fellow you'll ever come across." The descriptions are endless. But can you see how important it is for others to see God's Spirit resting upon you more than any of these other things? That's not to diminish your life; it's instead to elevate it by drawing on the power of God's presence that can elevate you.

I don't know what opportunities will come your way or how you will have the chance to represent yourself to people. But if after leaving their presence they can say of you, "Now, there's someone whose life bears evidence of the Spirit of God," then be certain that regardless of what they think, God will be impressed even more.

It Doesn't Get Better Than This

Psalm 133:1

How good and pleasant it is when God's people live together in unity!

Our world, and especially our country, is so divided today. The middle ground on most matters has been taken up by people on both sides on the spectrum so that you must choose which side to land on or keep your mouth shut.

But there is a third option: Try to get along with those you may not see eye to eye with, as a way of bearing witness to your desire to turn down the heat on some of these conversations that are on the verge of boiling over and burning down our civility with it.

So, how can you do that with integrity? How can you stay connected with people you might have disagreements with without compromising your own soul in the process? You look for things that you do agree on and your focus on them.

In Psalm 133, the Psalmist celebrates how good and pleasant it is when God's people dwell together in unity. I doubt seriously that the people of God were always in agreement back then any more than we are today. It's just that the Psalmist wants God's people to offer an example of the joy of those who come together under God's name and commit themselves to serving his purposes.

Sometimes you turn on the news, throw up your hands, and ask, "Is there anything we can agree on?" If we make the things of God the primary concern in every aspect of our life, then we can indeed throw up our hands, not in frustration and exasperation, but in effusive praise. Because when God's people come together, it doesn't get any better than that.

A Circle for Everyone

Acts 15:7-11

After much discussion, Peter got up and addressed them: "Brothers, you know that some time ago God made a choice among you that the Gentiles might hear from my lips the message of the gospel and believe. God, who knows the heart, showed that he accepted them by giving the Holy Spirit to them, just as he did to us. He did not discriminate between us and them, for he purified their hearts by faith. Now then, why do you try to test God by putting on the necks of Gentiles a yoke that neither we nor our ancestors have been able to bear? No! We believe it is through the grace of our LORD Jesus that we are saved, just as they are."

There's a famous line penned by the poet Edwin Markham that goes like this? "He drew a circle that shut me out—heretic, rebel, a thing to flout. But love and I had the wit to win. We drew a circle that took him in."

Sadly, the circles most people draw today are the kind that do shut others out; that's human nature. When people don't look like you nor share your background nor see life as you do, shutting others out comes quite naturally. But that "love" part that takes people in? That's not natural; it's supernatural—the work of the Holy Spirit.

In Acts 16, the church has come to what sociologists today would call a "tipping point." In other words, depending on how the church decides on what to do with the Gentiles, the cause of Christ can progress or decline.

The vast majority of early believers were Jewish, having accepted the apostles' testimony of how Jesus was the promised Messiah. There were a few God-fearers such as Cornelius who had come to faith in Christ, but now these non-Jews are coming to faith in Jesus in droves, causing some in the church to feel overwhelmed.

So, the apostles hold a conference in Jerusalem to determine the matter: "Do we shut these Gentiles out, or do we take them in?" (The fact that you and I are a part of the church today should be all the evidence you need to know that they made the right call. Otherwise, we would be shut out—on the outside looking in.)

Simon Peter stands up at a high moment at the conference and seals the deal on the inclusion of the Gentiles with these words: "We believe that it is through the grace of our LORD Jesus that we are saved, just as they are." In other words, the one thing that brings us all together is the body of Christ—not what we have or know or do. It's the grace of Jesus that draws a big-enough circle to let us all in, at least those of us who desire to do so.

Think about that today as you bump into people who some would call "EGRs" (Extra Grace Required). Make sure your circle is big enough to include them and not so small to shut them out. In fact, if you make it a circle that's more the shape of a cross, then there will surely be enough room: it will be you and Jesus. "But love and I had the wit to win. We drew a circle that took him in."

Waiting and Hoping

Psalm 130:5

I wait for the LORD, my whole being waits, and in his word I put my hope.

I recently took one of those tests that seeks to gauge the level of your emotional health. It's a part of a study group I had agreed to be a part of, and I guess that I wanted to know if I was emotionally fit to participate. I could tell that most of the questions had to do with my level of hopefulness. In other words, how do I look at my life today? More importantly, how do I anticipate my life going forward? Am I hopeful about the future, or am I thumbs down, or somewhere in between?

Well, I scored high on the hopefulness scale. Part of that is my personality, but part of it is because of where I put the source of my hope. I'm not hopeful because of my own strength or ingenuity. I'm instead hopeful because of my confidence in God.

I think that's how people of faith best look to their future. Certainly, we see that truth in Psalm 130, where the Psalmist encourages God's people "to wait for the LORD...and put their hope in Him. For with the LORD there is unfailing love and with him there is full redemption." God doesn't fail us when we fail him. In those moments God reaches down to us and sees us through to the good future he has for us to know.

These are times when I see people who have given up hope. That's because they've looked everywhere but to God for a reason to be hopeful about tomorrow. Don't make that mistake. Too much is on the line. Even when you find yourself facing the most severe of life's tests, look to God and you will pass your spiritual health test. You will graduate to that good future God has for you to know.

He Is Willing

Matthew 8:1-3

When Jesus came down from the mountainside, large crowds followed him. A man with leprosy[a] came and knelt before him and said, "LORD, if you are willing, you can make me clean." Jesus reached out his hand and touched the man. "I am willing," he said. "Be clean!" Immediately he was cleansed of his leprosy.

Most of us have been brought up not to "put others out." You know what I mean by that expression. You don't want to impose on other people. You don't want to be a burden to them. So, if there's something you need them to do for you, you learn how to approach them without making them feel obligated in any way. You say something like, "If it's OK with you," or "if you're not doing anything else." The point is, we don't want to presume upon their grace.

Sometimes that attitude spills over to our relationship with Jesus. It's almost as if we think there are only so many times when can approach our Savior for his grace and then he might hate to see us coming. "Here comes Doug again. I wonder why he can't help himself."

That's not how Jesus thinks about us. We see that in Matthew 8, where a man with leprosy approaches Jesus and asks him if he would be "willing" to make him clean. And how does Jesus respond? "I am willing. So, be clean." The beauty of that healing story is that Jesus always has time for everyone regardless of how many times those persons approach him.

Jesus always has time for you. So, if today you find yourself in need of his help for the first time or the 15th time or the 5,000th time, Jesus will be happy to see you coming his way. He is most willing to do for you what you could never do for yourself.

Boast in the LORD

2 Corinthians 10:17-18

But, "Let the one who boasts boast in the LORD."
For it is not the one who commends himself who is approved,
but the one whom the LORD commends.

People who boast tend to rub us the wrong way, do they not? That's because their unduly high estimations of themselves keep them from seeing and celebrating the good in other people. Their view of themselves always being at the center of their universe just won't let them. So, when we see these types coming, our first impulse is usually to see if we can go the other way.

But there is a form of boasting that actually has the potential to cause others to move closer to us, and that's the boasting that magnifies the difference the grace of Jesus makes in our lives.

In 2 Corinthians 10, the Apostle Paul talks about the need for Jesus followers to "boast in the LORD." This second letter to the Corinthians was a tough one for Paul to write. A good number of people in the church at Corinth weren't all that big on Paul. Some even said that he seemed full of himself. So, Paul answered their criticisms by helping them to understand that if his confidence caused any of them to bristle, then they should understand that it wasn't a self-confidence Paul possessed. It was a confidence in Christ, one that all believers would do well to have.

I've always thought that there's a thin line between confidence and conceit. But we can make the line wider by representing whatever confidence we do possess as stemming from the spirit of Jesus in us. Then, when others see the difference Jesus makes, not only will they move toward us, but hopefully they'll move toward Jesus and find in him the grace that will grant them the confidence they need.

The Peril of Judging Others

Romans 2:1

You, therefore, have no excuse, you who pass judgment on someone else,
for at whatever point you judge another, you are condemning yourself,
because you who pass judgment do the same things.

One of the worst experiences of my young life was serving as a judge at high school "beauty review." You remember those events; don't you? I was in college and single, and when approached to come in at the last moment as a substitute judge by a friend who was serving in the Baptist church there, I thought it would be a great way to spend a Saturday night. Boy, was I wrong!

I don't know that I have ever been subjected to such pressure by parents and friends, as along with the other two judges, we would enter and leave the room between sessions. I promised God that if he would get me through that fiery furnace, I'd never volunteer to enter it again.

We might think that being in a position to judge others is a good thing, something that affords us a chance to analyze people from a loftier perch. But the truth of the matter is that when we find ourselves doing it, it never turns out like we thought it would. We find out it inevitably hurts other people when our judgments don't point out the beautiful in other people.

But it also hurts us, as the Apostle Paul explains it in his letter to the Romans. According to chapter 2, when we judge others, in the process we place ourselves under the same microscope we use to analyze them—at least in God's eyes. It's usually the case that the very things we condemn in someone else are the things we most wrestle with ourselves. We just try to deflect the attention away from ourselves to others, but God sees and God judges.

If today you come across someone that you feel the need to judge, hit the pause button and think twice before you do. Make sure that what you feel the need to judge in them isn't something that troubles you about yourself. Most importantly, try instead to see them in the same way God sees both them and you. Then trust in the grace that God makes possible in Jesus Christ so that you can feel better about the other party, and you can also feel better about yourself.

An Incomprehensible Puzzle

Romans 11:33-36

Oh, the depth of the riches of the wisdom and knowledge of God! How unsearchable his judgments, and his paths beyond tracing out! "Who has known the mind of the LORD? Or who has been his counselor?" "Who has ever given to God, that God should repay them?" For from him and through him and for him are all things. To him be the glory forever! Amen.

To improve their brain functioning, a lot of folk work puzzles. It may be a crossword puzzle or a word or numbers game. The idea is that by engaging with these various puzzles, we exercise our gray matter and stay as sharp as possible.

But have you ever come across a puzzle you couldn't solve and you just gave up on it? You did the best you could, but it wasn't good enough. We've all come across "puzzles" that for us are unsolvable.

That's how the Apostle Paul felt as he reflected on God's faithfulness to God people in his letter to the Romans. In chapters 9–11, Paul seeks to reconcile God's covenant promises to Abraham with God's provision of Jesus Christ. The dilemma Paul sees becomes so confounding that he throws up his hands, though not in despair but instead in effusive praise. "Who has known the mind of the LORD?" he concludes. "To him be the glory forever."

You'll surely run across some "puzzles" in life that you won't be able to solve. But if you discover they're beyond you, have the faith that they're not beyond God. In fact, God has already solved them his gift of Jesus Christ, for from him and through him and to him are all things. To him be the glory forever.

A Call Too Close to Consider

Psalm 124:1-5

If the LORD had not been on our side—Israel say—if the LORD had not been on our side when people attacked us, they would have swallowed us alive when their anger flared against us; the flood would have engulfed us, the torrent would have swept over us, the raging waters would have swept us away.

Have you ever had a close call in life, one that when you looked back on it, caused your soul to wobble at the tragedy of what might have been? Some people relish those kinds of situations. What was it Winston Churchill once said? "Nothing in life is so exhilarating as to be shot at without result?" The close calls I've had in my life are ones I really wouldn't care to repeat, and I would imagine you feel the same way.

The Psalmist sure does, at least as he explains his reflections on life in Psalm 124: "If the LORD had not been on our side, our enemies would have swallowed us alive and the raging waters would have swept us away." In other words, no reasonable person should ever be deceived into thinking that he can make it through this life without some help from above. The threats are too severe. The dangers are too great.

But when you face the threats and dangers that come your way with the power that God makes available to those who trust in him, nothing will take you down or do you in. As the Psalmist invites us to believe, our helper is the very maker of heaven and earth. Nothing is impossible for God.

Consider that promise today as you go about your life. If you will, you'll not only look back to yesterday with a sigh of relief for not having to endure what might have been; but you'll also look ahead with the same sigh of relief because of what possibilities with God on your side lie ahead. Nothing is impossible for God. If you look to him, it will stagger you what will be possible for you.

Walk in the Way of Love

Ephesians 5:1-2

Follow God's example, therefore,
as dearly loved children and walk in the way of love,
just as Christ loved us and gave himself up for us
as a fragrant offering and sacrifice to God.

If there's anything that should characterize our witness as Jesus followers, it should be the way we walk in love. That's how Paul phrased it in Ephesians 5.

Non-believers in the first century were impressed by the initial followers of Jesus by "the way they loved one another." But today, our situation demands that we broaden the scope of our love to include everyone we cross paths with. So, how do we do that, when we inevitably have to contend with people we find unlovely?

The place to begin is by understanding that the love the Bible speaks about isn't mere emotion. That's how our culture defines love, but in the Bible, love is something you do. In particular, love in the Bible involves wishing for the best and working for the best for everyone. And then you give of yourself in ways that can make that happen.

If you need a model for how that giving works, Paul tells us there's no better one than Jesus. When we give of ourselves in love, we're being imitators of the Christ who gave himself for us.

So, today if you run into someone you don't like, much less love, try to see them as Jesus sees them. Follow his lead, and work for their very best. It may surprise you at how much better they start looking to you. And it may surprise them about how much they see the presence of Jesus in you.

He Will Be Overthrown

2 Thessalonians 2:7-8

For the secret power of lawlessness is already at work; but the one who now holds it back will continue to do so till he is taken out of the way. And then the lawless one will be revealed, whom the LORD Jesus will overthrow with the breath of his mouth and destroy by the splendor of his coming.

Sometimes you look around and it seems as if the powers and principalities are having their way in everyday life. Nothing seems to be adding up. Everything seems to be spiraling out of control. Crash and burn appear to be the order of the day.

Christian faith, however, has never resigned itself to a dualistic view of life, as if evil and good are on the same level. Instead, Jesus followers have always chosen to believe that the good Jesus came to bring into this world will ultimately prevail, even if it often appears otherwise.

In 2 Thessalonians 2, Paul unpacks this weird disconnect between what our faith emphasizes and what the reality around appears to be. For these believers to whom Paul was writing, wrestling with the evil in their world wasn't a theoretical exercise; it was something they faced in real life. And they wanted to know they were on the right side.

Paul's words assured them that they were, and they should not be deceived. Evil will be doomed for destruction. God's good in Christ Jesus will prevail. Faith trusts in that promise regardless of how improbable it sometimes appears to be. That's what Paul means when he encourages the believers to live in "love of the truth."

Today, I encourage you to do the same. Then whatever difficulties you encounter will not get the best of you, not when God has already given you his best in Jesus. Trust your difficulties to him and know that your life will be in very good hands.

Finish Strong!

Revelation 3:2

Wake up! Strengthen what remains and is about to die,
for I have found your deeds unfinished in the sight of my God.

There are many people who are great at starting things but lousy at finishing them. That's because getting started on something is energizing and exciting. But when it's something that demands discipline and focus, many give up when the going gets tough.

According to the Bible, that's precisely what being about God's work is like. It's exciting and invigorating, but it also requires your ongoing dedication—which is why for many their initial devotion often flags and fizzles.

In Revelation 3, the Spirit challenges the church at Sardis to "wake up and strengthen what remains and is about to die, for I have found your deeds unfinished in the sight of my God." Clearly, believers in that church were allowing their struggles and challenges to deflate their zeal for what God had given them to do.

Maybe the same thing is happening in your life. The challenges of this present season have gotten the best of you, even though you want God to have the best of you. If that's the case, then trust in the power of the Holy Spirit to do what you will never do on your own—strengthen your zeal and awaken your devotion—so that "he who began that God work in you may bring it to completion." Only then will you know the everlasting life Jesus wants you to know and be a part of a work, both in your life and in the world, that will never die.

Wide Open

Revelation 3:6

I know your deeds.
See, I have placed before you an open door that no one can shut.
I know that you have little strength,
yet you have kept my word and have not denied my name.

Nothing is more frustrating than to find yourself facing a locked door. How many times have I gotten up and gone out to pick something up, only to have arrived at the store before it was opened? When that has happened, I've been presented with two options: turn around and go home or stay there until the owners decide to open. Both options clearly involve a change of plans.

In recent days and months, we've encountered a lot of locked doors. This COVID virus has resulted in a good bit of changing of plans and lost opportunities at every turn. And yet, all the while God is still very much at work. We just have to learn how to direct our attention and adjust our plans accordingly.

In Revelation 3, the Spirit addresses the church at Philadelphia. It's the only one of the seven churches in Revelation that doesn't receive admonishment or condemnation. But what they do receive is the promise of an open door, one that no one will ever shut. For these believers, God makes possible a way for them to keep pressing forward in the face of the dangers they must contend with and to press forward with the confidence that God will see them through.

Today, God will see you through. He has set before you an open door. In a season where everything at times seems to be closed, what God opens for us is something most definitely worth pursuing.

Yielding Ears

Exodus 7:14-16

Then the LORD said to Moses, "Pharaoh's heart is unyielding; he refuses to let the people go. Go to Pharaoh in the morning as he goes out to the river. Confront him on the bank of the Nile, and take in your hand the staff that was changed into a snake. Then say to him, The LORD, the God of the Hebrews, has sent me to say to you: Let my people go, so that they may worship me in the wilderness. But until now you have not listened..."

How well do you listen? Your answer likely depends on whether the information being shared with you is something you find interesting or relevant. There's so much noise in our world that we have come to find it necessary to practice "selective listening." I hear what I want to hear, and what I don't want to hear I ignore.

So, where does God rank in the realm of voices you pay attention to? A lot of that likely depends on how open you are to being changed. God's word always evokes change, and when we don't want to change, we don't give God the ear God deserves. But you do know how dangerous that is; don't you, given how God's word is always in your best interest?

In the book of Exodus, God is preparing to convince Pharaoh, king of Egypt, to let God's people go from their bondage. As God speaks to Moses about his plans, Moses raises the concern that Pharaoh won't listen to him. God, however, is not deterred. In chapter 7, God says, "Until now, Pharaoh has not listened, but soon he will." That's because God will soon unleash a series of plagues that will command Pharaoh's attention—plagues that Pharaoh will not be able to ignore.

Some days I feel like we're living in the midst of a plague with this coronavirus; don't you? Maybe this is the perfect time for us to start paying even more attention to God. It may be that until now we haven't been listening to God very well either. But in this day when everything is changing and nothing will remain the same, perhaps we should. Whatever God has to say will certainly be in our best interest and move us forward into the promised future God has for us to know.

First Things First

1 John 3:16

This is how we know what love is:
Jesus Christ laid down his life for us.
And we ought to lay down our lives for our brothers and sisters.

One of the more interesting aspects to me of how people think is our obsession with lists. We enjoy ranking things whether they be restaurants or movies or sports teams or books. And of course, the ones we value more than the others are those we rank number one. Everything else on our lists is in a position where they are looking up on number one.

We carry this tendency over into our everyday life in terms of our priorities. We may not actually write them down because we don't have to. They're inscribed upon our souls, and everything we say and do are driven by what we believe to be our number-one priority in life.

So, how does that work as a Jesus follower? All of life must be directed to our devotion for Jesus, and everything we say and do should reflect our commitment to him. John, one of Jesus' first disciples, speaks to this essential in his first epistle, where he spends a good bit of time emphasizing the importance of love. "This is the message you heard from the beginning. We should love one another." And when pressed to give an example of what that love looks like, John proceeds to answer: "This is how we know what love is: Jesus Christ laid down his life for us."

Evidently, Jesus thought enough of you and me that he would make that kind of sacrifice. So, the surest sign of our faith in him is our willingness to show that same love to others. As we do, we bear witness to the abundant life to which Jesus calls us.

So, today, if you find it hard to keep everything in your life in the right order, start with love. Claim the love Jesus has shown you, and then channel it in everything you're about with respect to others. Then it won't just be an ordinary life you will live; it will be life in all its abundance.

Be Careful What You Hear

Romans 10:17

Consequently, faith comes from hearing the message,
and the message is heard through the word about Christ.

Some years ago, I was privileged to have been the pastor of one of the sweetest souls you'd ever want to meet. She was caring and tender and about as accepting a person as I had ever met. But over the course of weeks and months, I saw a dramatic change in her attitude. She had become critical and suspicious. Her soul had somehow closed up to the needs of others around her. As I listened, it became apparent what had produced the change. Her days were being spent listening to talk shows that traffic in anger, and the steady drumbeat of antipathy had taken its toll on her.

We become what we pay attention to, which can also be a good thing if we direct our attention to what points us in the direction of Jesus. That was Paul's counsel to the Romans in chapter 10, which is that part of the letter where Paul pleads with his own people to give ear to the proclamation of the gospel of Jesus Christ.

"Faith comes from hearing the message and the message is heard through the word of Christ." In other words, our hearts are changed as we give our attention to the truth about Jesus—his love for us sinners, his invitation to follow him, his promise to lead us to life. There would be no way for us to experience any of these aspects of salvation if it were not for the opportunities that have come our way to hear, to believe, and to be changed for the better.

Some voices you will be able to turn off; others won't be so easy. But if in every voice you filter what you hear through the word about Christ, whatever changes you undergo will be changes for the better.

Live Good and Glorify God

1 Peter 2:11-12

Dear friends, I urge you, as foreigners and exiles, to abstain from sinful desires, which wage war against your soul. Live such good lives among the pagans that, though they accuse you of doing wrong, they may see your good deeds and glorify God on the day he visits us.

Everyone is a people-watcher. We're all watching one another and making judgments on the values that guide our behavior. I don't mean that we necessarily watch others to criticize them; we just pay attention to how others live so that we can figure out what makes them tick. That's because talk is cheap. But watch how someone behaves, and you'll learn as much as you care to know about them—even if they never speak a word to you.

So, how does your life speak? That was a question Simon Peter emphasized to believers in the first letter he wrote to the churches for which he was responsible. Many interpreters have called 1 Peter an instruction manual for new believers, and in chapter 2 he wants his readers to understand that people who don't know Jesus will be paying close attention to their behavior. In particular, they will want to see the difference Jesus is making in them.

Two thousand years later, that part hasn't changed. People are still watching to see if there's anything different about us. Therefore, Peter's words are as relevant for us today as they were for Christians in his day: "Live such good lives…that they may see your good deeds and glorify God on the day he visits us." Live in such a way that others see the marvelous difference that the presence of Jesus makes in you. Only then will they be convinced that our words have validity because of how they see evidence in the good that Jesus empowers us to do.

Remember that someone today will be watching you. So, give them something to talk about, something that might turn them in the direction of Jesus where they can know the full and meaningful life Jesus awakens in all who live for him.

God's Gracious Watch

Psalm 121:5-8

The LORD watches over you—
the LORD is your shade at your right hand;
the sun will not harm you by day, nor the moon by night.
The LORD will keep you from all harm—he will watch over your life;
the LORD will watch over your coming and going both now and forevermore.

Nothing is worse for us humans than to feel as if we're ignored. It's better that people disagree with us than ignore us. At least that tells us that we're showing up on someone's radar screen. But of course, it's much better for others to take notice of us in a good way.

According to the Psalmist, that's precisely how God looks upon his human creation. God takes notice of us and watches over us in the very best of ways. In Psalm 121, we are reminded of how "God watches over our comings and our goings, both now and forevermore." In other words, there never is a time when God is not watching over us, and he does so always with our best interest at heart. The only question is, Do we live in the confidence that nothing we do escapes God's attention? Or does that thought bother us, as if we have something to hide?

Clearly, the intent of the Psalmist is to assure us that we have nothing to fear with God's gaze keeping watch over us. If anything, we can rest calmly in the knowledge that God does so to help us and protect us and bless us. And if God sees anything in or from us that would cause him displeasure, he has already provided for that as well by granting us his mercy and grace through our faith in Christ Jesus, which enables us to be certain of God's support going forward.

So, today, if you feel alone or forgotten, know that you are not. God is watching over you to do you great good.

Subject Index

Scripture Index